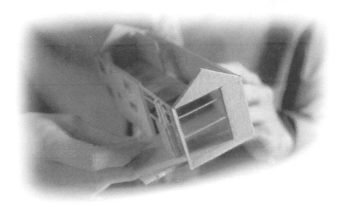

BUILDING A GODLY HOME

God's Blueprint for Men

D0289039

WOODROW KROLL

Foreword by Gary Oliver

BACK TO THE BIBLE®
Publishing

BACK TO THE BIBLE PUBLISHING
P. O. Box 82808
Lincoln, Nebraska 68501

Editors: Allen Bean, Rachel Derowitsch
Cover design: Laura Poe
Cover photo: Eyewire Inc.
Interior design: Laura Poe
Art and editorial direction: Kim Johnson

Additional copies of this book are available from Back to the Bible Publishing. You may order by calling 1-800-759-2425 or through our Web site at www.resources.backtothebible.org.

Previously published under the title *Is There a Man in the House?*

ISBN: 0-8474-1461-2

Printed in USA

DEDICATED TO
CHOSEN MEN,
MIGHTY MEN OF VALOR,
WHO PURSUE GOD
FEARLESSLY,
RELENTLESSLY,
TOTALLY.

CONTENTS

Foreword

Only a generation ago our society was a lot clearer on what it meant to be a man. Gender roles were much simpler. Men did certain things and women did certain things. A man's identity was in what he did, how he performed, and how much money he made. I'm not saying that was healthy or right. That's just the way things were.

Today circumstances have changed dramatically. The questions have changed. The rules have changed. Many men are no longer sure of what it means to be a man. The questions men are facing today are much deeper and more complex than ever.

One of the most basic questions many men are asking is, What does it mean to be a man? Everybody seems to have their own idea of what a man should be and do. For example, what do you think of when you hear expressions such as, "He took it like a man," "Act like the man of the house," or, "Are you a man or a mouse"? What characteristics come to your mind? Where did you learn them? What are they based on—the standards of our society, the clear teaching of Scripture, or both? Are they as valid today as they were twenty years ago?

In Ezekiel 22:30 God said, "I looked for a man among them who would build up the wall and stand before me in the gap on behalf of the land so I would not have to destroy it, but I found none" (NIV). What was true then is still true today. God is still looking for men who have the character and courage to stand in the gap. And the good news is He's finding some.

Hundreds of thousands of men across the United States and around the world are acknowledging their emotional, relational, and spiritual bankruptcy and coming back to God and back to the Bible for the hope and healing they so desperately need. In unprecedented numbers men of different ages, ethnic backgrounds, and denominational affiliations are looking up and reaching out for truth that can make a difference in their lives.

For years many men have been little more than human hamsters on the treadmill of production and performance. We have been human do-ings rather than human beings. We've lost sight of what it means to be a man. We've lost touch with the priorities that should mark a man who is becoming conformed to Christ. We've allowed the tyranny of the urgent to blind us to what is truly important.

In *Building a Godly Home: God's Blueprint for Men*, Dr. Woodrow Kroll takes these and other issues head-on. He addresses some of the key concerns facing Christian men today. With candor and courage he challenges us to reevaluate our roles, rethink our priorities, and redefine our purpose in light of the clear teaching of God's Word. He shares timeless truths that can help and encourage you to move beyond a performance motivation to a maturity motivation.

If the desire of your heart is to be a man whom God can trust, if you want practical help in how to build a godly home by growing as a lover, leader, protector, worshiper, priest, provider, counselor, disciplinarian, and encourager, then this book is for you.

—Gary J. Oliver, Ph.D.
Siloam Springs, Arkansas

Introduction

WHAT IS A MAN?

In her *Good Housekeeping* column, "The Way We Are," Lois Wyse wrote about a young boy who was asked by a neighbor, "And what do you want to be when you grow up?" He thought for a moment and then answered, "A female forklift driver."

In this unisex and androgynous age, who can blame the boy if he got a little mixed up? Many grown men also struggle with who they are and what role God wants them to fulfill in regard to their wife and children. They are not sure of their identity, let alone their place in God's plan. With all the gender blending, blurred responsibilities, and conflicting definitions, trying to figure out what it means to be a man can be perplexing.

Some men, even Christian men, feel that the male gender could qualify for the endangered species list. Statistics indicate that men in the United States have a shorter life expectancy than women—a little more than seventy-three years (compared with eighty for women). Also, men are twice as likely to die of a heart attack, adolescent males are seven times more likely to become mentally ill, and suicides among men are four times more prevalent.

If nature has not been kind to men, neither has society. The plight of the male population seems ordained to be an uphill battle. As one wit says: "When he is born, his mother gets the congratulations, candy, and flowers. When he is married, his wife gets the parties, publicity, and gifts. When he dies, his widow gets the life insurance. Life is not fair!"

Men also run a greater risk of being murdered, robbed, and assaulted than do women. Of course, some of this may be their own fault. There's a lot of pressure on men to live up to Hollywood stereotypes that frequently put them in harm's way in places like bars, on the streets, and even in their homes. Men appear to have a knack for courting disaster.

Dr. Gary Oliver says, "Today's man is a cardboard Goliath, unable to flow with the changing social scene. We've been reduced to work machines, performers and bread winners. We've been sold a bad image of manhood. And we've paid for it with our health, with our emotions and with our relationships."[1]

In the United States there also appears to be a growing antagonism toward men. Patrick Arnold, author of the book *Wildmen, Warriors and Kings*, claims, "A new kind of prejudice called 'misandry' (the hatred of males) is beginning to appear in many circles."[2] Certainly men have been targeted by the more militant of the feminists. Gerald Bray goes so far as to say that "the radical wing of the feminist movement has made the destruction of male society a specific policy goal."[3] While that may be an overstatement, it is evident that during the last decade the male image has been seriously damaged.

It seems everyone knows what a man should be except men themselves. Television—the chief shaper of modern opinion—tells us a man is someone with fresh breath (from using the right toothpaste), no dandruff (from using the right shampoo), and aggressively macho (from driving the right pickup). The corporate world tells us a man is someone who is impeccably dressed, stylishly successful in his BMW, and married to the company first and his wife second. Yet women say they want their men to be softer, gentler, more sensitive, and attentive to their needs. Who is a man to believe?

In his book *Dad the Family Coach*, Dave Simmons observes, "Men are baffled by the conflicting role expectations shouted at them from different authorities. In our culture, there no longer exists a specific universal concept of the role of the adult male in the family. Men are confused because they can't find a clear job description and instruction manual. Many men have gotten out of step not because they march to the beat of a different drum, no one beats the drum for them at all."[4] How can the man of the house determine the role he should assume? Who will teach him the way to build a godly home?

The good news is that there is an instruction manual that can answer this question, if men will only read it. It's called the Bible, and like all good manuals, it is written by the Maker of the product. Genesis 1:27 says, "So God created man in His own image; in the image of God He created him; male and female He created them."

In the days when the automobile was first becoming popular, a man purchased a brand-new Model-T Ford. He drove it proudly onto a busy street, where it promptly stalled. No matter how hard he tried, the owner could not get the newfangled contraption started. Just as he was about to give up, a chauffeured limousine pulled up behind him and a wiry, energetic man got out. "Let me give you a hand," he said. After tinkering with the Model-T for a few moments, the smartly dressed man said, "Try it now." The man did and the car started at the first crank. "How did you know what to do?" the owner asked in amazement. "It's not hard when you know these cars as well as I do," the stranger replied. "I'm Henry Ford."

The omniscient God who created the family and established the husband as the head of it is more in touch with what it means to be a real man than any physician, psychologist, feminist, philosopher, or TV producer. Furthermore, He has some specific things to say in His instruction manual concerning what He wants men to be. Knowing who you are and how you are supposed to run your life is easier when you allow your Maker to provide the directions.

Today many women are wondering if there's truly a man in their home. They don't mean the kind of man our society often considers a "real" man. They aren't interested in the macho Don Juan with the Hollywood image. Such men may be popular on the afternoon soap operas, but they don't wear well in real life.

Most women aren't impressed with the guy who thinks he looks good with rumpled clothes and a two-day stubble. A slob by any other name is still a slob. Sensible women also refuse to settle for the sports-addicted beer guzzler who lives only for the weekend. They know there is more to life than preparing snacks for halftime and cleaning up the mess after the game.

Understandably, women want a real man—a man who knows what it means to be a man.

God, too, is looking for real men. In 2 Chronicles 16:9 the prophet Hanani says, "For the eyes of the LORD run to and fro throughout the whole earth, to show Himself strong on behalf of those whose heart is loyal to Him." God is actively seeking men whose hearts and behavior are consistent with the plan He created for them. To decipher the design of that plan, today's male first has to wade through a multitude of myths about what it means to be a man.

THE MYTHS OF MANHOOD

Abraham is an outstanding example of both a man's man and God's man. As the youngest son of his father, Terah, a descendant of Noah's son Shem, Abraham grew up in Ur of the Chaldees, a large metropolis in Sumeria. In the beginning his name was Abram (meaning "Father is exalted"), but God changed his name to Abraham ("Father of a multitude") in Genesis 17:5 after He promised that Abraham would have a son.

Eventually, Abraham moved with his father and family to the city of Haran. There his father died, and God called Abraham to step out in faith to "a land that I will show you" (Genesis 12:1). Abraham took his wife, Sarah, and his nephew, Lot, and began a journey that continued for the rest of his life.

Abraham never gave a law like Moses, never sang a song like David, never composed a proverb like Solomon, never uttered a prophecy like Isaiah, and never wrote a book like Jeremiah. Still, he is known as "the father of all those who believe" (Romans 4:11) and as "the friend of God" (2 Chronicles 20:7; Isaiah 41:8). How did he become such a man?

Physical strength

Abraham must have been a man of great strength. As far as I know he pumped no iron, ran no ten-kilometer races, nor spent three afternoons a week working out in the gym. Still, his first journey took him from Ur of the Chaldees to Haran. Ur was located in southern Mesopotamia about halfway between the Persian Gulf and the present city of Baghdad. Haran was in northwestern Mesopotamia. Almost five hundred miles separated these two cities. Yet Abraham didn't jet between them; he didn't drive an SUV from one city to the other; there were no trains or buses. In all likelihood he walked or rode a camel. It was an arduous journey, yet he made it.

Later God spoke to him again. This time the call was to leave Haran. "Now the LORD had said to Abram, 'Get out of your country, from your kindred and from your father's house, to a land that I will show you. I will make you a great nation. I will bless you and make your name great, and you shall be a blessing. I will bless those who bless you, and I will curse him who curses you; and in you all the families of the earth will be blessed.' So Abram departed as the LORD had spoken to him, and Lot went with him" (Genesis 12:1–4).

What is perhaps most remarkable about this story is that Abraham was seventy-five years old when he left Haran to explore an unknown land. At a time when most men are seeking a rocking chair, Abraham was seeking a new country five hundred miles away. Moreover, it was no less of a challenge than his first trip. Obviously he was still a man of incredible physical stamina. He probably could have wrestled men half his age and won, but that was not what made him a man.

You may think you have to stand six feet, six inches and have a body as hard as a rock if you want to be a real man. But that's a stereotype, not the truth. The Bible does not condone the neglect of bodily conditioning. In fact, it says that "bodily exercise profits a little," but it never says it makes you a real man.

Strength, size, physique, and muscles are all part of the macho male image, but don't let that deceive you. Physical strength may make you strong, but it doesn't make you a man.

World travel

Others view men of the world—world travelers—as the real McCoy. They think, *If only I could travel to faraway places and bring back exotic stories of my escapades, then I would be a real man.* But this, too, is just a tantalizing myth.

Abraham certainly traveled the world, to the extent it was known to him. Genesis 12:6 reveals, "Abram passed through the land to the place of Shechem." Later he moved from Shechem to the mountain east of Bethel (12:8). From there he journeyed south and finally down into Egypt.

At one time or another Abraham lived near at least five exotic cities: Shechem, Bethel, Hebron, Beersheba, and Gerar. He also traveled about in Egypt. Yet nowhere does the Bible indicate that this made him a man. In fact, it seems whenever Abraham journeyed very far from Canaan, he got into trouble.

Genesis 12:10–20 says that he went to Egypt because of a famine. Fearing that the Egyptians would kill him and take his beautiful wife, Sarah, he convinced her to tell them she was his sister. He said, "Please say you are my sister, that it may be well with me for your sake, and that I may live because of you" (v. 13).

Abraham deliberately plotted to deceive the Egyptians in order to save his own hide. When Pharaoh heard reports of Sarah's beauty, he took her into his harem. Fortunately, he learned the truth (that she was Abraham's wife) and returned her to her husband. This duplicity, however, earned Abraham an escort to the border with the implication he would not be welcome to return (vv. 19–20).

Not only did Abraham tarnish his testimony in Egypt, but it was probably during this time that he procured Hagar, whose name meant "fugitive" or "immigrant," as a servant for Sarah. Genesis 16 reveals the problems this liaison created. Abraham fathered a child by Hagar and named him Ishmael. Later he fathered a child by Sarah and called him Isaac. Ishmael is the patriarch of the Arab nations, and Isaac is the patriarch of the Jewish nation, Israel. To this day, Israel and her Arab neighbors coexist in a state of uneasy peace sometimes broken by outright war.

In another instance Abraham traveled toward Egypt but stopped short on the southern border of Canaan at a city called Gerar (Genesis 20). Again he lied about Sarah, and she was taken into the harem of Abimelech, the king. God warned Abimelech in a dream not to touch Sarah because she was Abraham's wife. Had Abimelech not obeyed, he surely would have been struck dead for his transgression. Terrified, Abimelech returned Sarah to Abraham, but not without a strong rebuke for his behavior. How sad that a pagan had legitimate grounds for censoring a believer.

Does travel make the man? Ask Abraham. It almost broke him. No, real men are not men of the world, roaming the planet looking for adventure. If anything, travel presents temptations that compromise a man's ability to be the kind of witness God wants him to be.

Unlimited wealth

Some believe that the depth of your portfolio or the size of your bank account determines your manhood. This philosophy is reflected in the bumper sticker that says, "The man who dies with the most toys wins!" These men live by a philosophy that assumes if you could simply amass enough cash, create a sizeable portfolio, or purchase an expensive house, then you would be a real man. Women would beat a path to your door, while other men would envy you. But is this true?

Abraham was a wealthy business tycoon. In his day he would have been a Fortune 500 guy, topping *Forbes* magazine's annual list of the wealthiest men in the world. Genesis 13 reveals that he was not only prosperous, but he had successfully diversified his holdings. He owned a great many livestock, so much that sufficient grazing land wasn't available for his herds and his nephew's herds. In addition to cattle, Abraham possessed a small fortune in silver and gold. He was a well-heeled individual indeed, but nowhere does Scripture indicate that this made him a real man.

The Hilton is one of the greatest hotel chains in the world. Entrepreneur Conrad Hilton, who founded and built this empire, gave his family name to the enterprise. Mr. Hilton was a wealthy man, but he also knew that money was not the answer. On his calling card he had a short story that he called "Food for Thought." This is what it said:

In 1923, a very important meeting was held at the Edgewater Beach Hotel in Chicago. Attending this meeting were some of the world's most successful financiers. Those present included the president of the largest utility company, the president of the largest gas company, the greatest wheat speculator, the president of the New York Stock Exchange, a member of the President's cabinet, the head of the world's greatest monopoly and the president of the Bank of International Settlements.

Certainly we must admit that here were gathered a group of the world's most successful men. At least, men who had found the secret of making money. Twenty-five years later let's see where these men are:

The president of the largest utility company—Samuel Insull—died a fugitive from justice and penniless in a foreign land; the president of the largest gas company—Howard Hospson—went insane; the greatest wheat speculator—Arthur Cutten—died abroad, insolvent; the president of the New York Stock Exchange—Richard Whitney—was recently released from Sing Sing Penitentiary; the member of the President's cabinet—Albert Fall—committed suicide; the president of the Bank of International Settlements—Leon Fraser—also committed suicide.

All of these men learned well the art of making money, but not one of them learned how to live.

Some of the greatest men in history possessed little material wealth. George Whitefield, known for his open-air meetings and evangelistic fervor, once said, "I make no purse. What I have, I give away. 'Poor, yet making many rich' shall be my motto still." Yet Whitefield went down in history as one of the most influential leaders of America's Great Awakening (1725–1760).

Not only did Jesus not have a penthouse apartment, He actually had no place to lay His head (Matthew 8:20). It wasn't simply that His personal holdings were not vast, He was so poor he had to borrow a boat (Luke 5:1–2), a donkey (Matthew 21:2), the upper room (Mark 14:14–15), and even a tomb in which to be buried (Matthew 27:59–60). Yet He was the greatest man who ever lived.

THE "O" WORD

If manhood is not measured in terms of strength, travel, or wealth, what else is left? When we study the Bible, the answer to what makes a real man is quite evident.

Abraham was man enough that even God called him a friend. The key to Abraham's manhood, however, was not any of the superficial trappings that the world thinks is so important—it was his obedience.

Obedience is a struggle for both men and women. Seemingly, however, women have a greater sensitivity to spiritual issues. Over the years I have observed that if only one parent in the home goes to church, chances are it is the mother. This leads me to conclude that men stand in greater need to develop in this area of obedience—particularly those who want to be real men.

Jesus said that we can have the same privilege as Abraham. Every man who lives in obedience to the will of his Heavenly Father proves himself to be a friend of God and a real man. Jesus told His disciples, "No longer do I call you servants, for a servant does not know what his master is doing; but I have called you friends, for all things that I heard from My Father I have made known to you" (John 15:15). But prior to that He made clear the basis for this friendship: "You are My friends *if you do whatever I command you*" (v. 14).

By Jesus' own words obedience is the true test of manhood. John MacArthur Jr. said, "Don't throw God a bone of love unless there's the meat of obedience on it." Jesus said in John 14:21, "He who has My commandments and keeps them, it is he who loves Me. And he who loves Me will be loved by My Father, and I will love him and manifest Myself to him."

Real men know that obedience is a sign of maturity; disobedience is for those who are yet children. Cindy Johnson shares the story of her four-year-old son. One night she found him sobbing in the hallway. Concerned, she asked him if he was hurt. "No," the little boy replied, "Daddy said a bad word to me!" Knowing that there must be some misunderstanding, she probed, "Honey, what bad word did Daddy say?"

Seeing the possibility for sympathy, the little boy stopped crying and blurted out, "Obey!"[5] In the eyes of a child, whether four or forty, *obedience* is a dirty word.

Obedience in the face of difficulty

Only a real man can handle the rigors of obedience. There's no room for sissies, even if those sissies can bench-press a car. The conditions for obedience involve some tough challenges. Yet obedience requires that we do our duty even if we fear the consequences.

A Roman soldier was given a message to deliver as quickly as possible. He was advised that the fastest route would take him through a territory where he stood a good chance of losing his life. His reply was, "It is not necessary for me to live, only to obey." That's what a real man would say!

The well-known commentator Alexander McClaren wrote, "If we do our duty, God will see to the consequences." Our concern is not for the degree of difficulty; our concern is to make sure we obey.

Obedience in the face of confusion

Furthermore, obedience requires us to do our duty even if we do not understand why. The famous nineteenth-century preacher Philip Brooks summed it up well when he said, "We don't understand God's will and then obey it; we obey God's will and then He gives us understanding." Many things are difficult to comprehend, especially for men these days. So often we say, "If I were God, I wouldn't do it this way!" But bear in mind the two axioms made famous by Alcoholics Anonymous: 1) There is a God; and 2) You aren't Him.

In her book *Tramp for the Lord*, Corrie ten Boom tells of the time God called her to Argentina. She argued, "But I've never been to Argentina. I can't speak a word of Spanish. Air travel is poor, and flying across the Atlantic Ocean to Buenos Aires will be a trying ordeal."

God still said, "Argentina." So she went. When she and her traveling companion arrived they were exhausted, and the gentleman they expected to meet at the airport was not there. No lodging, no sponsor, and no meetings were scheduled. Her companion said, "Tante Corrie, are you sure that God's guidance brought us to Argentina?"

A few moments later a man recognized her. When he discovered that Corrie was there to minister but her sponsor had failed to show up, he offered to introduce her to a woman doctor who was a Christian. The doctor provided lodging and soon arranged for numerous meetings. One of these meetings was in the ward of a local hospital that specialized in polio patients. Corrie met a Jewish man there confined to a rocking bed. When the bed rocked up he could breathe in; when his head went down he breathed out. Corrie shared the Gospel with him, and he accepted Christ as his Messiah. Within minutes after she left him he died.

During her weeks in Argentina, multitudes of men and women came to know Christ as their Savior and were strengthened in their faith—all because Corrie was obedient in the midst of uncertainty and confusion.[6]

If you want to be a real man, a man of God, a man who is the friend of God, your responsibility is to live your life the way God wants you to and let Him take care of the "whys." You aren't God, but without obedience to Him you aren't much of a man either.

FACING THE STORMS

In 1992 Hurricane Andrew hit southern Florida, leaving an estimated $12 billion in damages, fifty people dead, and thousands homeless. A TV news crew was filming this devastation when they came to a neighborhood where all the homes were flattened except for one. The owner was outside cleaning up his yard, so the crew stopped and asked, "Sir, why is your house the only one still standing? How did you manage to escape the severe damage of the hurricane?"

"I built the house myself," the man replied. "I also built it according to the Florida state building code. When the code called for two-foot by six-foot roof trusses, I used two-foot by six-foot roof trusses. I was told that a house built according to code could withstand a hurricane. I did, and it did. I suppose no one else around here followed the code."

When the sun is shining and the skies are blue, building your life on something other than the guidelines in God's Word can be tempting. But there's a hurricane coming—for everyone. Only men who build their lives obedient to God's standards will weather the storm.

In the following chapters, let's see what standards God expects us to obey.

[1] Dr. Gary Oliver, *Masculinity at the Crossroads* (Chicago: Moody Press, 1993), p. 13.

[2] Patrick Arnold, *Wildmen, Warriors and Kings* (New York: Crossroad Publishing Co., 1992), p. 1.

[3] Gerald Bray, "Friends or Lovers," *Christianity Today*, December 12, 1994, p. 47.

[4] Dave Simmons, *Dad the Family Coach* (Colorado Springs, Colo.: Victor Books, 1991), p. 19.

[5] Cindy Johnson, "A New Four Letter Word," *The Evangelical Beacon*, February 17, 1986, p. 11.

[6] Corrie ten Boom, *Tramp for the Lord* (Old Tappan, N.J.: Fleming H. Revell Co., 1974), pp. 99–103.

Chapter 1

THE LOVER IN HIS HOME

More than two hundred years ago a new edition of a well-known encyclopedia was published. The editors devoted four lines to the topic of the atom and five pages to the topic of love. A few years ago the editors of this same encyclopedia produced a new edition, in which they devoted five pages to the atom and left out love completely.

This typifies a disconcerting trend in our society. In the midst of advancing technology, we have lost the concept of what it means to love. Some people are so caught up with their cell phones, computers, and PDAs that they fail to concentrate on people. A conversation overheard in a restaurant illustrates our predicament. The husband was questioning, "Honey, what do you mean, 'we don't communicate'? Just yesterday I faxed you a reply to the recorded message you left me on your answering machine."[1] No wonder businessmen say their lives are empty.

The Palo Alto Consulting Center in California conducted a study of 4,126 male business executives. Forty-eight percent said that despite years spent striving to achieve their professional goals, their lives seem meaningless. Sixty-eight percent of senior executives admitted they had neglected their families to pursue professional goals, but half of those questioned also confessed they would spend less time working and more time with their wives and children if they could do it over again.

Men are particularly vulnerable to getting caught in the job trap. Their identity becomes synonymous with their employment. Often men see their value only in terms of their contribution to the company. The higher up the corporate ladder they climb, the more worthwhile and important they feel. They put blinders on and see only their work. Some neglect their relationships with their wives and children to the point of ruin. Perhaps that's why God specifically addressed husbands in Ephesians 5:25, "*Husbands*, love your wives, just as Christ also loved the church and gave Himself for it," and again in verse 28, "So *husbands* ought to love their own wives as their own bodies; he who loves his wife loves himself."

God views men differently from the way many of them view themselves. He doesn't identify them by their job. He doesn't see a man as a "suit" or a "jock" or any of the other popular stereotypes. He sees men as compassionate lovers of their wives and children. He singles out men to be the lovers in their home.

The key to your responsibility to be the lover in your home lies in loving your wife. One young teen said, "I wish my parents knew that unless they truly love each other, there is little they can teach their children about the love of God." She is right. Before a man can properly love his children, the family dog, or even the pet gerbil, the man of the house must first learn to love his wife.

Many people look at Ephesians 5:22–24 and lament the hard lot God has given the wife to submit to her husband. But the following verses (25–33) lay what arguably could be an even greater responsibility upon us men—to love our wives and, through our wives, to love our family. That's why you need to heed what God's Word says about how you are to love that special woman in your life.

SACRIFICIAL LOVE

Paul's admonition to the Christian men of Ephesus is that the lover in the home is to love with a sacrificial love. In our society we don't hear much about sacrifice—especially between husbands and wives.

A newspaper in Indiana reported that a widow brought in a lengthy copy of her husband's obituary. The obituary writer told her they would be glad to publish it, but it would cost twenty-five cents per word. "In that case," she said, "just print, 'Sam Brown dies.'" The writer informed her that there was a seven-word minimum for a death notice. Mrs. Brown pondered the situation for a moment and finally said, "Well, then, print, 'Sam Brown dies, '88 Ford for sale.'" Some spouses have failed to grasp the concept of sacrifice!

Jesus understood sacrifice very well. He made many sacrifices long before He sacrificed His life on Calvary's cross. His trail of sacrifices began when He left heaven and all its glory to come to earth in the form of a humble man. That wasn't Jesus' coming out party; it was His coming down sacrifice. Dottie Rambo's words ring true: "He left the splendor of heaven . . . if that isn't love the ocean is dry, there's no stars in the sky, and the sparrow can't fly!"

Until we actually see heaven, we can't fully appreciate what Jesus gave up when He agreed to be born in a human body. The beauty of heaven escapes our imagination. John describes the New Jerusalem, the city of God, in Revelation 21 as having walls of jasper and streets of pure gold (v. 18). The foundations are adorned with all kinds of precious stone (v. 19), and each of the twelve gates is carved out of a pearl (v. 21). As beautiful as it sounds, I suspect John was able to tell only half the story. Heaven surpasses the expression of human words.

But heaven is more than a beautiful location; heaven is also a place of fellowship. When He left heaven, Jesus sacrificed those intimate, face-to-face meetings with God the Father and God the Holy Spirit. On earth He would commune with Them, but not in the intimate way He did in Their presence in the divine throne room. When we are absent from our family, we often feel a stabbing pain in our heart. Jesus was no different. Yet because He loved us, He was willing to bear that painful separation from the Father.

Then, of course, Jesus faced the necessity of death. That was His ultimate sacrifice and His ultimate expression of love. And it was no ordinary death. Death on the cross was one of the cruelest, most shameful ways to die. The cross was excruciatingly painful. But along with the pain there also was public humiliation.

Furthermore, Jesus died in every sense of the word. The Bible speaks of two types of death. One death simply means the body ceases to function. Everyone walks through that dark vale. The other death, however, is reserved for those dying in their sins. This results in separation from God. The Book of Revelation calls it the second death (20:6; 21:8). Jesus not only died in body, but He suffered separation from God too. As He took on the sins of the world, He was cut off from His beloved Father for the first time in all of eternity. If that's not sacrificial love, nothing is.

When a husband loves his wife as Christ loved the Church, he, too, must love sacrificially. A young man once met with his pastor to explain a problem. He said, "Pastor, I'm afraid I love my wife too much. She is always on my mind."

The pastor asked, "Son, would you be willing to die for her?"

"Well," the man answered slowly, "that's something I'd have to think about."

"Then, young man, your problem is not that you love your wife too much. You don't love her enough."

Most men today would have to think long and hard if they were asked to lay down their physical life for their spouse. But that would almost be easier than what they actually need to do—die to self in order to live for their spouse. The love of a husband for his wife is to be a compassionate and caring love, a love that demonstrates his concern for his wife, not just in dying for her but in living for her and seeking her welfare.

When George H. W. Bush was vice president of the United States, his wife, Barbara, described him in a public speech as one of the most caring men she had ever known. A woman replied, "My husband is the most caring man I know too. He cares about the Cubs, the Bears, the Bulls, and every other stupid sports show on TV."

Some women probably would have to be taken to the emergency room for resuscitation if their husband ever said, "Honey, I'm going to turn off this football game so we can spend a little time together." But I'm sure most women would be willing to take the risk.

Very few husbands will ever be called upon to die for their wives as Jesus died for the Church. But all husbands are called upon to care for their wives as Jesus cared for the Church. Husbands are to cherish their wives as Christ cherished the Church—so much that He was willing to die for it.

Tradition says that Cyrus the Great, king of Persia, captured a young prince and his family. The young man's life was in jeopardy, but Cyrus was a fair man. He asked the prince, "What will you give me if I release you?"

"Half of my wealth," the prince replied.

"And what if I release your children?" Cyrus questioned.

"Everything I possess," the prince said.

Once more Cyrus asked, "And what will you give me if I release your wife?"

Without hesitation the young man replied, "Sir, I will give you myself."

Cyrus was so taken back by the man's devotion to his wife and family that he released the prince without harm or payment. On the way home the prince remarked to his wife, "Did you notice how ruggedly handsome King Cyrus was?"

"No, I didn't. I only had eyes for you, the one who was willing to sacrifice everything for me."

No husband can say he truly loves his wife until he is willing to sacrifice for her. As someone has said, "You can give without loving, but you can't love without giving." Are you willing to make such a sacrifice?

SANCTIFYING LOVE

Furthermore, you must practice a sanctifying love. Ephesians 5:26 tells us that Jesus made His sacrifice in order that He might "sanctify . . . [the Church] with the washing of the water by the Word." To sanctify means to set apart for service. God commanded Moses to make special clothes for his brother, Aaron, and his sons, saying, "So you shall put them on Aaron your brother and on his sons with him. You shall anoint them, consecrate them, and sanctify them, that they may minister to Me as priests" (Exodus 28:41). Moses did not create the priesthood; God did. But Moses sanctified Aaron and his sons. He set God's chosen servants apart so they could function in that ministry to which God called them.

One of America's great national treasures is Mount Rushmore. Gutzon (John) Borglum worked from 1927 to his death in 1941 carving out the heads of presidents George Washington, Thomas Jefferson, Abraham Lincoln, and Theodore Roosevelt on this mountain in South Dakota. When someone asked how he produced such marvelous works, Borglum replied, "Those figures were there for forty million years. All I had to do was dynamite four hundred thousand tons of granite to bring them into view."

In the same way, the lover in the home makes sure that his wife is released at times from her domestic world to serve the Lord in whatever capacity He has called her. Her gifts are there; God gave them. You need to insure that the opportunity is provided and encourage your wife to use her gifts. That may mean playing "Mr. Mom" for a day. It may mean hiring a baby-sitter while she participates in a Bible study group. Whatever the case, husbands should consider it an expression of the sanctifying love they have for their spouse. You must give the woman of the house every opportunity to be all that God wants her to be. To deny that responsibility is to deny being the lover in the home.

As part of your sanctifying love, you also must seek to keep your wife separated from the world. That doesn't mean you keep her locked up in the house. Quite the contrary. The lover of the house assists her in keeping a godly perspective on the world around her. He discerns with her the world's philosophy so together they do not buy into it.

Some segments of our society loudly cry that unless a woman is liberated from the home, she can't possibly be fulfilled. It is easy to believe those lies when life consists of washing, ironing, cleaning house, and maybe holding down a job as well. But the lover in the home is responsible for freeing his wife to be the important person that she is. He helps her fight against the powerful social pressure seeking to press her into the world's mold either in the home or in the business world. Support your wife as she discovers that she has much to give in meaningful service to the Lord while at the same time enjoying the wonderful privilege of being a wife and mother.

INTIMATE LOVE

Anyone who owns a television knows the distorted view it projects of intimacy. If we were to accept Hollywood's warped perspective, we would believe the pathway to intimacy begins in the bedroom. But that's not true.

Josh McDowell tells of a phone conversation he had one evening with a young woman. She said, "Mr. McDowell, in the last five nights I've gone to bed with five different men. I got out of bed tonight and looked back and said to myself, 'Is that all there is to it?'" Between her sobs she said, "Please, sir, tell me there's something more!"

"Yes," Josh replied, "it's called intimacy. It's what the Bible means when it says 'the two shall become one.'"[2]

Intimacy begins with security. Security cannot be found apart from the committed relationship of marriage. Someone described a wedding ring as a band of metal around your finger that cuts off your circulation. That may be a backhanded compliment, but it's true. Intimacy requires the assurance that no intruders and no competitors will be allowed.

Within the context of marriage, the conjugal love of a husband and wife completes a sacred relationship. It's a physical union that parallels the spiritual union between Christ and His Church. The intimacy of the physical act symbolizes the intimacy that Christ will someday have with His Bride. In fact, Ephesians 5:27 says that the purpose of all Christ has done is "that He might present her to Himself a glorious church, not having spot or wrinkle or any such thing, but that she should be holy and without blemish."

There is nothing "dirty" about sex as God intended it. It has always been a beautiful part of His plan even before the Fall. We soil and defile it only when we take it out of the context God intended for it—marriage. Yet when sex is portrayed on television or in motion pictures, it is rarely between married partners. Hollywood has mastered the art of glorifying what God has forbidden and forbidding what God has glorified.

First Corinthians 7 gives guidelines for sexual conduct between a husband and his wife. The apostle Paul says, "Let the husband render to his wife the affection due her, and likewise also the wife to her husband. The wife does not have authority over her own body, but the husband does. And likewise the husband does not have authority over his own body, but the wife does" (vv. 3–4).

Paul recognizes that both men and women have needs that can be met best through an intimate, physical relationship. That relationship is normal, healthy, and created by God. What God designs should be enjoyed within the parameters He designates. In fact, Paul goes on to say, "Do not deprive one another except with consent for a time, that you may give yourselves to fasting and prayer; and come together again so that Satan does not tempt you because of your lack of self-control" (v. 5). The only responsibility that has a higher calling upon our physical body is our spiritual duty.

When a team of researchers from the University of Chicago completed the most thorough survey of sexual behavior in America since Alfred Kinsey conducted his more than fifty years ago, they were surprised at some of the results. One of those surprises was that the group of women who experienced the most fulfillment in conjugal love was conservative Protestants.[3] If the principles found in the Bible for governing the sexual relationship between husbands and wives are understood and practiced appropriately, they compose the best marriage manual you can buy. Enjoying sexual love within marriage should be the norm for all who wish to please God.

FRIENDSHIP LOVE

The love you have for your wife, however, needs to go beyond sexual love. You also must love her as a friend. The Associated Press reported the results of a survey that asked men, "What's the most important thing in your life?" One would assume the answer would be career, fame, or fortune. Surprisingly, 63 percent said it was their wives, and 90 percent of married men called their wives their best friend.

Lowell Lundstrom shared a study involving one hundred thousand married couples. The study indicated that the passionate physical love lasts an average of two years. If the husband and wife are not good friends at the end of this time, the marriage will likely die.[4]

Keep in mind that your friendship with your wife is like a bank account. You can put in and you can take out; but if you take out more than you put in, you're in trouble. Too many men have overdrawn their account. They need to find positive ways to increase the balance. Here are some suggestions:

Never complain. Consider what it would cost if you hired someone to come in and do all the things a wife usually does out of love. In the average family, the wife probably functions in many of the following roles:

Role	Hours/Week	Rate/Hour	Value
Childcare Provider	4.5	$6.61	$29.75
Dietitian	2.0	$16.84	$33.68
Purchasing Agent	3.3	$13.00	$42.90
Cook	13.1	$7.81	$102.31
Dishwasher	6.2	$6.00	$37.20
Housekeeper	17.5	$5.47	$95.73
Laundress	5.9	$8.78	$51.80
Seamstress	1.3	$7.09	$9.22
Practical Nurse	.6	$12.95	$7.77
Building Enhancement	1.7	$11.00	$18.70
Gardener	2.3	$8.24	$18.95
Chauffeur	2.0	$7.48	$14.96
Administrative Assistant	2.0	$10.75	$21.50
TOTAL	**62.4**		**$484.47**

(These figures are based on what some institutions in the Midwest offer as starting wages.)

Most women I know would think this is conservative!

Never criticize. The essence of love is realizing that when two people get married, two bundles (not one) of imperfection come together. Forget this and you may find yourself in the position of the husband who told his newlywed bride, "Honey, if you don't mind, now that we're married I'd like to point out a few of your little shortcomings." "Not at all," she sweetly replied. "It was those few little shortcomings that kept me from getting a better husband."

Many marriages die from what is called "the death of a thousand cuts." Supposedly, captors in the Orient would sometimes kill their prisoners not with one fell blow but by making hundreds of small cuts. Eventually the victim would bleed to death. Many spouses kill their marriages in the same way. It's one small criticism here and another little jab there. The marriage doesn't blow up; it oozes to death.

Jesus said, "How can you say to your brother, 'Let me remove the speck from your eye'; and look, a plank is in your own eye? Hypocrite! First remove the plank from your own eye, and then you will see clearly to remove the speck from your brother's eye" (Matthew 7:4–5).

Never condemn. Condemnation goes beyond finding fault; it passes judgment. Such comments as, "You'll never learn to be a decent housekeeper," or, "You'll always be a lousy cook," not only devastate but they're untrue. No one knows what the future holds but God. Condemnation robs the spouse of the most essential ingredient for keeping on—hope. Without hope, the husband will find that his statements become self-fulfilling prophecies.

A friend has been defined as someone who walks in when the rest of the world has walked out. That's the kind of friend you need to be. Your job is to encourage, strengthen, and support your wife no matter what the situation is. A friend is able to accept the other person just as he or she is.

In the movie *Shenandoah*, Jimmy Stewart plays the part of a father caught up in the Civil War. A young Confederate soldier comes seeking his daughter's hand in marriage. He asks the young soldier, "Do you like my daughter?" The young man responds, "Oh, sir, I love her!" The father replies, "I didn't ask you that. I asked you if you like her."

Every woman needs a good friend, someone who likes her as well as loves her. The lover in the home should be the first one on her list.

RESPECTFUL LOVE

If your wife is a believer, you not only have a lover and a friend but a sister in Christ. Men frequently do not see their wives as chosen vessels of God, people for whom Christ died.

Peter advises, "Husbands, likewise, dwell with them with understanding, giving honor to the wife, as to the weaker vessel, and as being heirs together of the grace of life, that your prayers may not be hindered" (1 Peter 3:7). This means the husband must treat his wife with gentleness and respect. You need to treat your wife with the same thoughtful attitude you would show your sister.

Some men might say, "But you don't know my wife. She's twenty pounds overweight, dresses slovenly, and never keeps the house neat." No woman *wants* to be overweight, dress slovenly, and be known as a poor housekeeper. Deeper issues are involved, and one of them might be respect.

I read some time ago of a culture in which it was customary to give cows as a bridal price. The father of an attractive young girl might be offered as many as ten or twelve cows in exchange for his daughter's hand in marriage. One day the plainest girl in the village became eligible to wed. She always walked with her head down and her shoulders slumped. She seldom smiled and never laughed. No one was expected to offer much for the chance to marry her. Yet suitors did come. One offered a cow, another upped it to two cows, but no one wanted to give much more. Then the most eligible young man in the village came and said to her father, "I will give you twenty cows for the hand of your daughter." The father was astounded. Word spread through the village. The people had never heard of such a magnanimous offer and especially for a girl like that. Of course the father quickly accepted.

When the couple came back from their honeymoon, everyone did a double take. Was this the same girl? She looked like a princess. Her head was held high, a smile was on her face, and her whole body radiated beauty. She had been transformed by respect.

When F. G. (Buck) Rodgers, former vice president of marketing for IBM, was asked what made IBM such a dynamite company, he replied, "First of all, it's based on respect for the individual." If you want to put a little explosive power in your marriage, show your wife some respect.

Many women measure respect by the extent to which their mates listen to them. Unfortunately, some men fall far short in this area. Men excel in doing, but because they don't listen, they often end up doing the wrong thing.

Diane Bonet reported in *Entrepreneur* that a dispatcher made a $100,000 error simply by not listening. He was instructed to route a delivery of building materials to Portland. At that point he stopped listening and sent eight truckloads of material to Portland, Oregon. Its destination was supposed to be Portland, Maine.

Women commonly complain that their husbands don't listen to them. That's a problem shared by many others. It is said that President Franklin D. Roosevelt decided to find out how many people really listened when he spoke informally at social gatherings. At the next White House reception, he greeted each person with a smile and a handshake while murmuring, "I murdered my grandmother this morning." People automatically responded with such replies as, "How lovely!" or, "So glad to meet you!" Nobody, he discovered, was really listening to what he said until he got to a foreign diplomat at the end of the line. As he gave his greeting, "I murdered my grandmother this morning," the diplomat responded softly, "I'm sure she had it coming to her."

I fear that numerous men leave their wives in the morning not having heard most of what they said. I wonder how many could vouch with 100 percent certainty that she didn't tell him, "I murdered my grandmother last night." As an act of respect, you need to listen to your spouse. To show that you have listened, you also need to respond.

Real communication requires that information be sent *and* received. Only if the husband in the home responds can a wife tell if her message has been received. Most women are not looking for wit or wisdom; they just want confirmation they've been heard.

The man, as the lover in the home, is responsible for building up his wife. That can't be done unless you first respect her.

EXCLUSIVE LOVE

A study released in the fall of 1994 called "Sex in America" claimed that 94 percent of married people were faithful to their spouses in the past year.[5] Those are encouraging figures. God's intention has always been for there to be one man for one woman. God made Adam a wife, not a harem.

The not-so-good news is that the divorce rates are still much too high. The U.S. Census Bureau reported that there were 1,163,000 divorces and 2,384,000 marriages in 1997.[6] While a number of these divorces are among people who have been previously divorced, it implies that a lot of couples are bailing out of marriage instead of working through their problems.

Having divorced, they then turn around and marry someone else, hoping that a new person can meet their needs. What this really represents is serial polygamy. Even though someone might be faithful to the one he married, that "one" keeps changing. The lover in the home needs to seriously consider the advice of Henry Ford. Often asked the secret for his long and apparently happy marriage, his stock reply was, "I follow the same principle in marriage that I do in business—I stick with one model."

We must never forget that when marriages go sour, the children are as much victims as the wife and husband. Ryan and Lindsey Berdan, ages nine and seven, can vouch for that. They get to see their dad every Wednesday night for a dinner and video games at the mall. A wishing well is in the middle of the mall. Ryan commented, "We always throw a penny in and wish that Mom and Dad would get back together."[7]

Unfaithfulness and divorce not only take their toll on the spouses, they negatively impact the whole family. You, as the lover in the home, are chiefly responsible for keeping the marriage healthy. You should take every step necessary to see that you have a home to love for a lifetime.

GREATEST OF ALL

In her book *To Live Again*, Catherine Marshall says, "Every human being needs love. Most of our troubles spring from the lack of it. Like thirsty men in a desert, we perish without it."[8]

Every responsibility that the man of the house is given is important. But the job of being the lover in the home is vital. All the other functions build upon this foundation. The apostle Paul says, "Though I speak with the tongues of men and of angels, but have not love, I have become as sounding brass or a clanging cymbal. And though I have the gift of prophecy, and understand all mysteries and all knowledge, and though I have all faith, so that I could remove mountains, but have not love, I am nothing. And though I bestow all my goods to feed the poor, and though I give my body to be burned, but have not love, it profits me nothing" (1 Corinthians 13:1–3).

Let all other things lag, if need be, but don't fail to be the lover in your home. Yet keep in mind that love is only the foundation, not the structure. A foundation never fulfills its purpose unless something is built on it.

A few miles from our former home is a cement pad situated forlornly in the middle of an otherwise empty lot. Rumor has it that the owner dug the footings, poured the concrete, and then discovered he didn't have enough money for the superstructure. It's a great foundation—the pad is positioned nicely in relationship to the road; the cement is troweled smoothly. But it's worthless. No one can live there until the house is built.

A firm foundation is important, and the lover in the home provides such a structure. Now let's see how God expects you to build a home on that foundation in which your family can live.

[1] *Homemade*, Vol. 15, #10, October 1991.

[2] Josh McDowell, Moody Founder's Week, Chicago, Ill., 1986.

[3] Philip Elmer-Dewitt, "Now for the Truth about Americans and Sex," *TIME*, October 17, 1994, p. 68.

[4] Lowell Lundstrom, *Heaven's Answer for the Home* (Springdale, Pa.: Whitaker House, 1985), p. 21.

[5] Elmer-Dewitt, p. 70.

[6] U.S. Census Bureau, "Statistical Abstract of the United States," 1999, p. 110.

[7] David Van Biema, "Learning to Live with a Past that Failed," *People Weekly*, May 29, 1989, p. 80.

[8] Catherine Marshall, *To Live Again* (New York: Avon, 1976), p. 177.

Chapter 2

THE LEADER IN HIS HOME

In 1979, *TIME* magazine said of the state of leadership in our nation, "It sometimes appears that Americans in the '70s have developed almost a psychological aversion to leading and to being led." More than a decade later *TIME* reviewed that statement and assessed that not much had changed. The aversion to leadership remains in full force, and the problem exists not only in our nation but, perhaps more important, in our homes.

Even Christian men discover that one of their most difficult challenges involves knowing how to be the leader of their home. Men don't set out to fail in their leadership roles, but often they do despite good intentions.

WHO'S TO BLAME?

If you frequently fall short in your God-given role as head of the home, who's to blame? You certainly can't blame God. His directions for male leadership are part of His comprehensive plan for men laid out in His Word, the Bible. Unfortunately, we implement God's plan infrequently because of the contrary circumstances in our world. Perhaps it's people who discourage us, circumstances that hinder us, or our own fears and insecurities that prevent us from closely following God's plan for our life. If you are to take God's leadership assignment for you seriously, you need to know who or what is keeping you from fulfilling it.

What are some of the leading causes of men faltering as the leaders of their homes?

Themselves

Men must accept their share of the blame. Businessmen will pay hundreds of dollars to attend seminars to learn how to be better leaders in their field. Seldom do they have the same motivation to spend that kind of time and money to learn to be a better leader in their home.

Recently I saw a bumper sticker that said, "Complacency is America's biggest problem—but who cares!" I'm not sure it's America's biggest problem, but I am convinced that complacency among men is epidemic.

For most men, if the roof isn't falling down, then everything is OK. For some men, however, God allows the roof to collapse. Take the case of Dan. He was a laid-back, easygoing guy. With a demanding job as an attorney, he was more than willing to let his wife run the home—until his son took an overdose of painkillers. Doctors were able to save his life, but he is left with permanent liver damage. Now Dan is thinking seriously about his role at home.

It's tempting to point the finger at everyone and everything but overlook the primary culprit—men themselves. Through no one else's fault, we have allowed the situation to degenerate to its current low point. When we fail as leaders of our home, there may be contributing factors, but there is only one failure—us.

Lack of role models

Weldon Hardenbrook makes this rather biting assessment of masculinity in our society: "The lack of adequate models of American masculinity, the increasing numbers of passive and withdrawn fathers, and the feminized approach to the major areas of education have combined to produce modern males who are bastions of passivity and irresponsibility."[1] In other words, leadership is difficult for many men because they've never seen it in action.

This has affected all segments of society. In the secular world, big business and large corporations lament the loss of identifiable leadership. At no other time in recent memory have we had more books on leadership and more seminars on how to be an effective leader and yet produced fewer real leaders. The effect is also felt in Christian circles. Dr. Kenneth Kantzer wrote in an article for *Christianity Today*, "These days Christian organizations have quit looking for leaders. Even a moderately effective leader would satisfy them and they settle for mediocrity, grateful for a minimum of brilliance and a maximum of security."

Management guru Tom Peters says of leaders and leadership, "Leadership is many things. It is patient, usually boring, coalition building. . . . It is altering agendas so that new priorities get enough attention. It is being visible when things are going awry, and invisible when they are working well. . . . It is listening carefully much of the time, frequently speaking with encouragement, and reinforcing words with believable action."[2]

So much of what Peters says with regard to the corporate world relates directly to our domestic world. Men need to see their role in the family in the same terms as Peters sees their role in business.

The leader of the home builds a cohesive unit out of varied interests and age groups in the family. Peters calls that "coalition building." The leader sees that the new priorities set by his teens don't get lost in the old priorities of becoming a grown-up. He listens, encourages, and reinforces. But more than anything else, the leader of the home is visible when things are falling apart in the lives of his family. He is the glue that holds the family together. But when things are clicking along well, the leader steps back, encircles his family with his arms, and leaves the center stage to others.

When you fail to lead your home in the areas that Mr. Peters mentions for corporate entities, your family becomes a microcosm of the mess in which much of big business finds itself. In the business world, in Christian organizations, and in the home, we need men who will set the example of what it means to be a leader. Biblically based models of leadership are in short supply.

Eager mates

Perhaps another reason men sometimes fail in their role as leader of the home can be traced all the way back to the Fall of man. Genesis 3:16 records, "To the woman He said: 'I will greatly multiply your sorrow and your conception; in pain you shall bring forth children; your desire shall be for your husband, and he shall rule over you.'"

Some interpret the word *desire* in this verse to mean sexual desire. They understand that a woman's desire for her husband resulted when Adam and Eve disobeyed God. But this would make the intimate relationship between a husband and a wife the result of a curse. Those who follow this line of logic usually conclude that the physical relationship is ungodly.

Another difficulty with this interpretation crops up when we realize sexual desire was present before the Fall, not just after it. Even before Adam and Eve tasted the forbidden fruit, God commanded them to "be fruitful and multiply" (Genesis 1:28). Therefore, a better explanation is needed than this.

In Hebrew, the word *desire* carries with it the thought of "running over" or "overwhelming" someone or something. The same Hebrew word is found in Genesis 4:7, where God tells Cain, "If you do well, will you not be accepted? And if you do not do well, sin lies at the door. And its *desire* is for you, but you should rule over it." God tried to warn Cain that sin would take control of his life if he were not careful. Based on that understanding of the word, some commentators suggest that one consequence of the Fall has been a power struggle between husbands and wives.

An elderly man was recalling the early days of his marriage for the benefit of his grandson. "Yes, sir," the man said. "I remember distinctly as I carried my new bride across the threshold of our little house, I said, 'Darling, this is our little world.'"

"And you've lived happily ever after," the young boy suggested.

"Not exactly," the grandfather replied. "I'd say it's more like we've been fighting for the world championship ever since."

By our nature most of us want to be in control. When a woman gives in to the desire to take control in the marriage relationship, her husband, whom God has ordained to be the head of the home, frequently acquiesces. She gains the control she wants, but at the expense of her husband's leadership. As a result, neither spouse is really happy.

Furthermore, as children observe the example set by their parents, they assume this is the way it should be and repeat this relationship in their own marriage as adults. Thus, an unbiblical pattern of leadership in the home is passed down from generation to generation.

The greatest gift a wife can give her husband is the right to be the leader of the home as God meant him to be. Sure, he'll make mistakes. Everyone does. But being disobedient to God's will is the biggest mistake of all.

Ineffective spouse

Sometimes an unsaved or a spiritually immature husband cannot effectively assume his leadership role. What's a wife to do then? She can do four things.

First, close the gaps. Quietly, unobtrusively, humbly plug the holes in your family left by your husband's inability to meet his spiritual responsibilities. Eunice is an excellent example of this principle. Her husband was a Greek and probably an unbeliever (Acts 16:1). Obviously, he could not be the spiritual leader of their home. So Eunice modestly taught her son, Timothy, the Scriptures, which his father could not do (2 Timothy 1:5; 3:14–15). Subtly, she filled the gap.

Second, encourage your husband. Some husbands simply need a little motivation to become the leader God wants them to be. They need a wife who is not looking for an opportunity to assume leadership, but who will gently nudge them to take the initiative. Moses was the great leader of Israel. But Exodus 4 records an event where Zipporah, Moses' wife, nudged him to apply himself to the role. Her intent was honorable, even if her tactics were unusual.

Third, create a climate in which your husband can lead. Speak to him privately about having a family devotional time. Ask him to lead; promise to assist. If you have a discussion time, don't answer all your children's questions; refer some questions to your husband. Say, "That's what I've come to believe. What do you think, honey?" Create an atmosphere that fosters your husband's leadership potential.

Fourth, pray that God will make a leader out of your husband. Christians often do not use the most potent weapon they have against Satan— prayer. It's not that they have tried prayer and found it doesn't work; they haven't tried it at all. Then they wring their hands and wonder what to do. The answer is to pray. Pray that God will change your husband. Pray that the Holy Spirit will interest him in taking the leadership role in your family. Prayer works best when nothing else works at all.

Fear of failure

Men can't always blame their lack of leadership on their wives. There's more to the problem. Some men shy away from leadership because it involves responsibility. It means being the target for blame when things go wrong. Every leader needs to come to terms with the reality of failure. It happens to all of us, but it's never easy to take, especially for some men.

Stephen Pile, founder of the Not Terribly Good Club of Great Britain, compiled a book of failures he entitled *The Incomplete Book of Failures*. While Pile wrote tongue-in-cheek, he nonetheless makes the point that multitudes of people have failed and yet lived to tell about it.

For example, he relates the story of a circus performer appropriately named Janos the Incredible Rubber Man. His act involved being lowered from a trapeze with his legs twisted like a pretzel behind his head.

After a few moments of rolling around for the benefit of the audience, he would untwist himself and resume a normal shape.

In August 1978 the performance was going well until it came time to untwist. Despite his best efforts, he couldn't do it. The circus manager finally took him to the hospital, where doctors worked for almost an hour to get him back to his normal shape. After several weeks of recovery, however, Janos resumed his contortionist act—humbled but not defeated.

That's also the response of the great leaders of the Bible. Moses was not much of a leader until he spent decades in the desert herding sheep. He spent forty years in the palace of Pharaoh thinking he was somebody. Then he spent forty years in failure on the back side of the desert thinking he was nobody. Finally, he spent forty years successfully leading the Israelites and finding out what God can do with a "nobody."

The same was true with the man Moses mentored. Joshua rose to leadership in Israel when Moses died. He inherited all the challenges of leading a rebellious and somewhat fractured people. The first real test of his leadership came not in the thrill of victory at Jericho but in the agony of defeat at Ai. Joshua proved his colors but only after a significant loss of face. The man who can't handle failure is not ready to handle success.

Yet in our success-oriented society, many men deem failure as fatal. Some husbands gladly turn over the leadership of the home to their wives after a disappointing scuffle or two. It means less chance of falling flat on their face again. And many wives are eager to take the reins rather than prop up and support a defeated husband. That only adds to a loss of leadership in the home.

Misleading media

Television also must take its share of the blame for discouraging men from being godly leaders in the home. In some of the more popular sitcoms, Dad is often little more than a well-meaning wimp. He is portrayed not as a caring and wise father but as a bumbling idiot or worse. The TV and movie industries say they are only depicting life as it is, but this does not help a man become what God designed him to be.

Hollywood's portrayal of the head of the home makes it difficult for some women to fulfill the biblical admonition found in Ephesians 5:33: "Let the wife see that she respects her husband." If we believe television, the average father is not worthy of respect. He is unappreciated by his employer, manipulated by his children, and controlled by his wife. Certainly this is not God's view of the man's role in the home.

Unfortunately, the indoctrination into this view of fatherhood begins early. A popular book series for young children, the Berenstain Bears, teaches many good truths. Yet if a person looks closely at the Berenstain family (Papa Bear, Mama Bear, Brother Bear, and Sister Bear), he would find Papa portrayed as only a cut above the children. In fact, sometimes he is worse than the kids.

In *The Berenstain Bears' Not-So-Buried Treasure*, Mama teams up with Grizzly Gran (the grandmother) to cure Papa and the cubs from focusing on material wealth (in this case, hidden treasure) instead of the real wealth of relationships. Certainly that's a commendable goal, but in the process Papa comes across as a bad influence on the children and the most gullible of the group. Mama and Gran appear levelheaded and wise, while Papa appears as a buffoon. The lessons taught are important, but the father image takes a beating.

The news media contribute to this dilemma as well. Spousal abuse cases that make the front page are almost always about a husband abusing the wife. Admittedly, this is a more serious problem than the reverse. It merits the concern of all Christians. No woman should have to live in fear for her life or safety, especially from the man who vowed before God to love and cherish her. Yet the amount of publicity that surrounds these cases would lead us to believe that every husband is a potential wife beater. If that is true, there are no godly men left among us.

When you consider the opposition, the man attempting to build a godly home faces some pretty tough odds. There are few encouragements for him to become the leader God intended him to be. But regardless of the image the media may project, a real man must strive to be obedient to God's Word: "For the husband is head of the wife, as also Christ is head of the church; and He is the Savior of the body" (Ephesians 5:23). You have a divine assignment, and that assignment is to be the leader of your home.

THE LEADERSHIP MODEL

But don't misunderstand. As the head of the home, you are a leader, not a dictator. To understand the difference, consider the following contrasts: A dictator rules by fear and force. A leader leads by example and persuasion. A dictator demands conformity. A leader allows for diversity. A dictator strives to root out and squash any challengers to his authority. A leader seeks to develop the potential of those committed to his care.

You need to ask yourself, "Am I a leader in my home or a dictator?" If you find it difficult to answer that question, ask your family. They could probably tell you quickly.

God calls the husband to be a leader—but not just any leader. He calls him to be a servant-leader. If you have difficulty grasping the concept of a servant-leader, the Bible provides both a definition and an example in the Lord Jesus.

In Philippians 2:5–7, Paul instructs his readers, "Let this mind be in you which was also in Christ Jesus, who, being in the form of God, did not consider it robbery to be equal with God, but made Himself of no reputation, taking the form of a servant [the New American Standard translation says "bondservant"], and coming in the likeness of men."

Abraham Lincoln is another example of what it means to be a servant-leader. Prior to a crucial battle in the Civil War, he sent a command to Gen. George Meade to attack the retreating Confederate Army. He attached a personal note to the orders that read, "The order I enclose is not on record. If you succeed, you need not publish it. Then, if you succeed, you will have all the credit of the movement. If not, I'll take the responsibility." Lincoln knew that to lead, you first have to serve.

The bondservant choice

Slavery was a common institution in Paul's day. The economies of Egypt, Greece, and Rome were based on slave labor. Historians have estimated that one person in three living in Italy and one person in five living elsewhere was a slave.

People were sometimes forced into slavery through war or poverty. Others were slaves because they were born into slavery. Still others became slaves as a result of committing a crime. It was possible, however, for a slave to gain his or her freedom. A Hebrew slave was to be freed after seven years of service. Sometimes masters would free slaves as a reward or as an act of kindness. Other slaves were able to save enough money to buy their freedom.

On occasion, when a slave was offered his freedom he chose not to accept it. Perhaps he had come to love his master because he was treated with kindness, or maybe the slave did not want to be separated from his wife and family. If that were the case, he was brought before the elders and had his ear pierced with an awl against a door or post. This was done as a token of lifelong servitude. He became a willing slave to his master. He was not forced to be a slave; he chose to be a slave. He became known as a bondservant because he was bonded to his master by love.

Paul says that Jesus became a bondservant. He was not forced into slavery; He loved us so much He chose to be a slave. Jesus said, "For even the Son of Man did not come to be served, but to serve, and to give His life a ransom for many" (Mark 10:45). The Lord exemplified this truth at the Last Supper as He willingly bathed His disciples' feet. Jesus assumed the lowliest of household duties as an indication to His followers of the kind of leaders they should be. He didn't just talk about being a servant-leader; He practiced it. He was the kind of leader for His Bride, the Church, that the husband needs to be for his family.

Are you willing to serve voluntarily? You can feel obligated to fill your role out of guilt or fear, but a real bondservant chooses to serve out of love.

Reality, not theory

Someone once said that the devil doesn't care what our convictions are as long as we don't practice them. We can easily become like the psychology professor who was a bachelor. Whenever he saw a neighbor scolding her child, he would advise, "You should love your boy, not punish him." One hot summer afternoon, this pompous professor was patching some holes in his concrete driveway. Tired and thirsty, he put aside his trowel, wiped the sweat from his brow, and started toward his house for a glass of lemonade.

Suddenly, out of the corner of his eye, he saw the mischievous neighbor boy putting his foot into the fresh cement. The professor rushed over, grabbed him, and was about to spank the daylights out of him when his neighbor hollered, "Watch it, Professor! Remember, you should love the boy, not punish him!" At this he yelled back, "I do love him in the abstract, but not in the concrete!"

Leadership cannot be left to languish in the abstract; it must be made concrete. The key to bringing servant leadership out of the realm of theory and into the real world of our families is what Charlie Shedd used to call the "H" twins: humility and honesty.

SKIP THE PRIDE RIDE

Many people misunderstand humility. They associate it with weakness, allowing people to run roughshod over them. But humility is far different from that. Dr. Shedd defines it as the courage "to face up to the difference between what we are and what we ought to be."

Paul admonished the Christians at Rome, "For I say, through the grace given to me, to everyone who is among you, not to think of himself more highly than he ought to think, but to think soberly, as God has dealt to each one a measure of faith" (Romans 12:3). The word *soberly* in this verse means to have sound judgment. When you think soberly about yourself, you are not deluded by much of the machismo image men like to portray today. Conversely, a man who has sound judgment is not plagued with false modesty either. Rather, you have a realistic understanding of who you are and what your assignment is in the family.

William Carey is considered the father of modern missions. The man who spent his early years as a cobbler became one of the greatest linguists the Church has ever known. He translated parts of the Bible into as many as twenty-four languages in India. But Carey was a humble servant of the Lord. When he first went to India some people treated him with contempt. Once at a dinner party a distinguished guest, hoping to humiliate Carey, said loudly, "I hear, Mr. Carey, you once worked as a shoemaker." Carey responded humbly, "No, your lordship, not as a shoemaker, only a cobbler."

Carey made no pretense of being anything more than what he was. He was so focused on the needs of the people of India that he had little concern about his qualifications for leadership or his comforts as a leader.

The most difficult person to face is ourselves. We're like overweight people who refuse to look at themselves sideways in the mirror. As long as we look straight on, we can pretend that our problems aren't so bad. It's only when we show our silhouette that the real situation becomes obvious. No one likes to admit he might be guilty of pride, but it is a common problem with men. It takes a real man to admit it and deal with it.

The English Puritan John Flavel wrote, "They that know God will be humble, and they that know themselves cannot be proud."

Pride devalues people

Nothing kills male leadership as quickly as pride. It closes you off from the beneficial insights that others might offer to you or about you.

THE LEADER IN HIS HOME

A missionary once mentioned that in the language of the tribe he was working with, the word *pride* literally meant "the ears are too far apart." In our culture we would say that a husband who is proud has a swelled head. In either case, such a man can't hear properly—his head gets in the way. He misses out on the wise counsel God sends him through those around him.

Pride also keeps you from appreciating those around you. As someone once said, "A conceited person has one good point; he doesn't talk about other people." That may be true, but a good leader knows the importance of acknowledging the value of the people who support him. So does a man who wants to build a godly home.

Perry M. Smith is a retired Air Force major general and former commandant of the National War College, a professional school for military and civilian leaders in Washington, D.C. In an insightful article for *Nation's Business*, Smith wrote, "Leaders should get up in the morning thanking people; at noontime they should thank more people; before going home at night, they should thank still more. Thanking people is an important part of taking care of them, because it's taking care of their psychological health."[3]

If this is true in the military and the business world, how much more should it apply to our families. A true leader of the home cares for every member of his household. Proud men, on the other hand, are so wrapped up in themselves they have little time to see and acknowledge the needs or accomplishments of those around them.

You need to decide what's more important: preserving the dignity and authority of your position, or serving the needs of those God assigns you to lead. The answer may tell more about you than what you might wish anyone to know. If there is anything small, shallow, or ugly about us, giving us a little authority will most certainly bring it out.

Being a husband and a father gives ample opportunity for pride to bring out the worst in us. It's only by the grace of God, and the godly humility that comes from that grace, that you can lead as a servant and not as a lord.

Pride destroys others

Out of pride men do things that they would never think of doing in humbler moments. Our desire to appear macho sometimes makes us think we can do anything to anyone and get away with it.

While a student at the Lyons Academy, Napoleon Bonaparte wrote an essay on the dangers of ambition. Unfortunately, in later years his pride caused him to forget his advice. He began a war that brought about ruin and destruction for himself and his nation.

Many men face the same defeat today. Their worldly ambitions drive a wedge between their family and themselves and lure them deeper into a web of failure and sin. Business becomes an obsession. Home degenerates into just a staging area for his real life—out there. The man's presence at home is unfocused and unfulfilling to everyone. His leadership in the family is abdicated.

Pride in getting that big account or pride in the admiration of your buddies at work can hamper your relationship with your wife and family. Soon you lose sight of who you are at home as well as at work. You become proud of being the boss of the house rather than humbled by God's assignment to be the servant-leader of the home. Men need to remember the sage advice of the American preacher Jonathan Edwards: "Nothing sets a person so much out of the devil's reach as humility."

Pride is the primary weapon Satan uses to destroy the leadership of the husband in the home. He often blinds men to their true role as servant-leader. He deceives us into believing our role is something akin to a junior CEO, a direction-determiner, an order-giver, a quasi-benevolent tyrant. That's not the leader's role, not in God's design for men. Leaders are to lead by example, not by fiat. Only true humility will permit you to be such a leader in the home.

Pride destroys your spiritual life

Most of all, pride hinders our walk with the Lord. It is impossible to be the leader of the home (or anything else) without the wisdom and direction of God's Holy Spirit. Pride convinces us we don't need the Spirit's direction. It puts up a roadblock that prevents us from receiving divine instruction. It hamstrings us so that we cannot successfully perform as the leader God designed us to be. Jesus cannot fill us with His wisdom as long as we are full of ourselves.

Furthermore, pride makes you vulnerable to Satan's traps. It convinces you that you are invincible and need not be concerned about the devil's devices. Men are especially susceptible to this type of pride (Isaiah 14:12–14).

A friend of mine was convinced he would never be tempted to be unfaithful. Less than a year after he shared that confidence with me, he became emotionally involved with another woman. Fortunately, he had the maturity to end the relationship before it went any further.

The apostle Paul warns, "Therefore let him who thinks he stands take heed lest he fall" (1 Corinthians 10:12). Be especially careful in those things you think are your strengths. Often we are on guard in areas we consider weaknesses, but vulnerable in areas we believe are our strengths.

THE HONESTY CRISIS

Humility alone won't make you a good leader. It needs the twin virtue of honesty. Together they give birth to godly leadership.

Our nation is in an honesty crisis. One survey indicated that 91 percent of Americans lie routinely, while 36 percent claim they have lied about very important matters. The Stanton Corporation gave a written honesty test to nearly three million job applicants. It reported that up to 31 percent of those applying were not trustworthy, compared with 12 percent in the mid-1960s. In thirty years, the penchant for dishonesty more than doubled.[4]

Lying has crept into every area of our lives, including our families. In many homes it has become the accepted norm. Pastor George Munzing tells of a time he went to counsel a family about their son's drug use. The father was distraught as he described the impact of drugs upon his relationship with his son. He said, "The thing that bothers me most about his being into drugs is the fact that drugs have made him a liar."

Moments later the phone rang and the man's wife went to answer. She returned saying that the call was for the man. He told her, "Tell him I'm not home."

Pastor Munzing correctly observed that drugs had not made the boy a liar; the father had.

Lying's toll

Lying destroys the ability to lead. There are already too many examples of this truth, but none proves it more than the notorious political scandal Watergate.

On June 17, 1972, five men burglarized the offices of the Democratic National Committee at the Watergate office complex in Washington,

D.C. They left a trail that led back to some of the highest officials in America, including former U.S. Attorney General John Mitchell, White House Counsel John Dean, White House Chief of Staff H. R. Haldeman, and White House Special Assistant on Domestic Affairs John Ehrlichman. When taped conversations were found implicating the president, Richard Nixon, the House Judiciary Committee approved three articles of impeachment. Rather than face the almost certain consequences, Nixon resigned on August 9, 1974. He was the first United States president forced to such disgrace.

It was not so much Watergate itself that brought down the Nixon administration but the effort to cover it up by lying. Lying strikes at the foundation of leadership—trust. If you cannot trust a person to tell the truth, how can you trust his leadership?

If you assume the leadership of your family—one of only three institutions established by God—you must practice honesty at any cost. Dr. Madison Sarratt, who taught mathematics at Vanderbilt University for many years, would admonish his class before every test, "Today I'm giving two exams; one in trigonometry and the other in honesty. I hope you pass them both. Still, if you must fail one, fail trigonometry. There are many good people in the world who can't pass trig, but none who can't pass the test of honesty."

THE BOTTOM LINE

Leadership is a tricky business these days, especially in the family. But the bottom line is that being the godly leader of a family means being the best example of God you can be to your wife and children. If you are less interested in yourself and more interested in them, it will show.

Dad, what do your children see in you? What is your life demonstrating to them about God? He demonstrated His love for us in that while we were sinners, Christ died for us (Romans 5:8). Real leadership means your personal agenda becomes secondary and God's agenda for you and your family becomes primary. Are you more interested in your flock than you are in their fleece?

Being a servant-leader, a confident leader, a godly leader, being the man in your house means accepting with gratitude the assignment God has given you. You are His representative to your family. You are what

Moses was to the Israelites: their guide, their servant, their intercessor, their leader.

Someone has said that a true leader has two characteristics: He is going somewhere, and he is able to persuade others to go with him. Where are you going, Dad?

In Lewis Carroll's famous fantasy *Alice in Wonderland*, Alice asks the Cheshire Cat for directions. "Cheshire-Puss—would you tell me please, which way I ought to go from here?"

"That depends a good deal on where you want to get to," said the Cat.

"I don't much care where," said Alice.

"Then it doesn't matter which way you go," said the Cat.

The Cheshire Cat spoke the truth. Only when you know your destination is the direction important. As the leader of the family, you need to know where you are taking your family. Is it toward life and godliness? Will it lead to heaven? The next several chapters will help answer those questions.

---

[1] Weldon Hardenbrook, "Missing in Action: Our Leaders," *Business Week*, October 29, 1990, p. 118.

[2] Thomas J. Peters and Robert H. Waterman Jr., *In Search of Excellence* (New York: Warner Books, 1982), p. 82.

[3] Perry M. Smith, "Twenty Guidelines for Leadership," *Nation's Business*, September 1989, pp. 60–61.

[4] *USA Today*, January 9, 1992, p. D-4.

Chapter 3

THE TEACHER IN HIS HOME

Christa McAuliffe, the teacher-astronaut who was killed along with six others in the explosion of the space shuttle *Challenger* in 1986, once said, "I touch the future; I teach."

As one who spent twenty years in the classroom as a teacher, I know what she meant. It was exhilarating to see my students take what I taught them and go on to contribute something of significance to the future.

It was exciting to be there for their first "Aha" experience, to stand by when the light finally dawned, when the pieces of the puzzle fell into place, when the students' eyes glistened with the light of understanding. It's also exciting years later to watch as they achieve the honor and recognition they deserve in their chosen fields. That's when being a teacher means everything. What I taught so many years earlier finally touches the future.

When I became a father, I discovered I was a teacher at home just as much as when I was in the classroom. In fact, home was my greatest challenge. It was more difficult to teach my children than to teach college students. The ones you live with are always a teacher's toughest challenge and far more difficult to impress. Most students see only the professional side of their professors, but children see the human side of their fathers. They know we have feet of clay.

Yet the effort will be worth it all when someday I stand and hear Jesus say to my children, "Well done, good and faithful servants." As their teacher, I will have a part in that. I not only touch the future, but through my family I touch eternity.

The responsibility of being the teacher at home is immense. At school the subjects I taught dealt more with the present. At home I instructed my children in truths that not only concerned their lives now but the hereafter as well. In the classroom my students were working for a grade; at home my family was preparing for heaven. The difference between the two situations is enormous.

What you teach your children in the home concerning the Christian faith will strongly influence the decision they make about their eternal destiny.

Someone has observed that the Church is always just one generation away from extinction. God has no grandchildren. Each generation is responsible to make its own decision about Christ. The interaction we have with our young people by words and deeds will either help or hinder them as they make that choice.

Sunday school, church, and youth organizations are all good places to learn, but by far the best teaching takes place at home. Graduate students at the University of Chicago were asked where they learned their key beliefs on morals and religion. One might guess it was from Sunday school teachers or peers. Instead, the majority of them said it was from the conversations held around the dinner table at home. The teaching, both formal and informal, that occurs within your home touches the future much more than you might realize.

WHO IS RESPONSIBLE?

Many men give their wives the responsibility of teaching their children. This may happen for a variety of reasons.

Some say, "But my wife is trained for it. She's a professional teacher." In all honesty, some of the poorest Sunday school teachers I've met were school teachers. That doesn't mean they were poor school teachers. Rather, the technique involved in teaching children spiritual truths is different from what one would use to teach academic subjects, such as algebra or geography. Spiritual teaching is geared to change lives for eternity.

Spiritual truths can achieve this transformation only if they are anointed by the Holy Spirit, who is the true Teacher (John 16:13). Furthermore, these spiritual principles can take hold and grow only if watered with the prayers of those who care. Obviously there are professional teachers who take this approach in teaching spiritual truths. But don't assume because someone is a teacher by occupation that he or she is by default the best person to pass on the realities of the Christian life.

God isn't looking for training. The Pharisees were trained to an extraordinary degree. They would play such games as throwing darts at a manuscript. Whatever verse the dart struck would have to be quoted verbatim, or the one who threw the dart would lose. They knew their Scriptures backwards and forwards, but I wouldn't have wanted them to teach my children.

God looks for teachers who are open to the leading of the Spirit. If you have training, that's wonderful. God can use it. But the most important qualification God seeks is a humble and contrite heart that looks to Him for wisdom and guidance.

Other men say, "I don't have the spiritual gift of teaching." That's understandable; not everyone does. I would not recommend such a person seek a position as a Sunday school teacher. On the other hand, sometimes we have to do those things in which we are not gifted as a matter of responsibility. Since God has given you the role of master teacher in the home, He will also give you the resources needed to be that teacher.

In fact, inadequacy may be the best thing men have going for them. It requires them to trust the Lord to take their deficiencies and make them sufficient. The apostle Paul had a thorn in the flesh (probably a physical ailment) that kept him from ministering the way he wanted to. He appealed to God three times to remove the affliction, but Paul records, "And He said to me, 'My grace is sufficient for you, for My strength is made perfect in weakness.' Therefore most gladly I will rather boast in my infirmities, that the power of Christ may rest upon me" (2 Corinthians 12:9). In our inadequacies God finds a platform to demonstrate His sufficiency.

A few men are honest enough to admit, "I just don't have time." Yet not making time to teach your values to your children is a fatal mistake. If you don't have time to teach your children, there are others who will. The drug pusher will be glad to spend time with your child and teach him or her how to smoke pot or snort cocaine. The pedophile will be more than happy to take the time to build a caring relationship with your young son or daughter in order to lure him or her into an illicit relationship. The local gang leader will eagerly fill the spot you leave empty and instruct your child in the way of protecting his turf.

Let's face it—the great paradox of time is that no one ever has enough of it, yet everyone has all that there is. All of us have exactly the same amount—twenty-four hours in a day. Some do not have more while others have less. The difference lies in what we choose to accomplish in the time God gives us. Our priorities determine how we use those precious hours. The man of the house who will not take the opportunity to teach godly values to his children has the time; he just doesn't have the commitment.

Some time ago it was reported that a supersonic airplane shot itself. The plane was moving so fast that it caught up with the bullet it had discharged. If you are moving so fast that you don't have the time to teach your children, you also might be in danger of shooting yourself.

Saying your wife is much better than you as a teacher is not a compliment but a rationalization. It's making an excuse for a lack of commitment. Saying you don't have the gift of teaching may be the truth, but underneath is a lack of faith. It says that you do not believe that God can work in spite of your limitations. God has spoken through everything from angels to donkeys; He can surely speak through you. Even admitting you don't have the time to teach your children isn't a confession; it's a cop-out. It's an excuse for mixed-up priorities.

The best thing for you to do with these rationalizations, half-truths, and excuses is to trash them. Even if they seem valid on the surface, they actually reflect a lack of trust in what God is able to do.

THE BIBLICAL MANDATE

God always desires the betterment of those who love Him and are called by His name. When He commands that something be done, neglecting to do it is to your detriment. It might be scary, it might be difficult, but it's always for your good.

God knows that those who are well versed in His Word and are obedient to it will avoid many of the pitfalls of life. Home is the best place for this teaching to take place.

The Bible says plainly that the man, the head in the home, is responsible for teaching his family. "And you, fathers, do not provoke your children to wrath, but bring them up in the training and admonition of the Lord" (Ephesians 6:4). Not pastors, not Sunday school teachers, not missionaries but fathers are commanded to educate their children.

The responsibilities

A critical analysis of biblical truth helps us to flesh out what Paul meant in this admonition to the Ephesian men. The specifics of a father's responsibility are found in these "dos and don'ts."

The Don'ts

Ephesians 6:4 specifically says, "Do not provoke your children to wrath." Instruction must be built upon the appropriate foundation. Anger and frustration do not provide an environment conducive to learning spiritual truths. Be sensitive to the behaviors that can unnecessarily provoke your children. Evaluate whether you need to avoid any of the following.

Avoid inconsistency. Charles Dickens once wrote, "In the world of little children, the greatest hurt of all is injustice." Unpredictable home situations produce a sense of injustice. The hurt from what is perceived as unfair leads to anger and rebellion. In that sort of environment, there is no hope to pass on eternal truths.

The man who wants to build a godly home needs to take great care that he is consistent in both his words and deeds. If you make a promise, you must keep it at all costs. If you espouse a position, make sure that your life mirrors what you teach. You need to model the truth as well as teach it. Albert Schweitzer once said there are only three ways to teach children: the first way is to model it, the second way is to model it, and the third way is to model it.

We can make all sorts of excuses for being inconsistent: "I'm so busy I should not be expected to remember." "I'm just the impulsive type." "I'm the original absentminded professor." But that does not make any difference with children. They, too, are masters at making excuses, so they know one when they see it. And they seldom accept it anymore than adults do.

Avoid narrow-mindedness. A man once bought a radio, tuned it to his favorite channel, and then pulled all the knobs off. He had no intentions of ever changing the station.

The dirtiest word in the English language for many people is *change*. The cartoon character Agatha Crumm is depicted as saying to her financial lieutenants huddled around her, "I don't mind progress. It's change I don't like."

Some young people feel their parents are opposed to change (any change), and they may be right to a certain degree. It's hard for the older generation to comprehend the transformations that impact our children. When I went to school, we rode a yellow school bus in from the country to our city school. I had little to fear. Occasionally a scuffle would break out, but it was broken up in minutes and forgotten in hours.

But today's school kids have to fear for their lives. In April 1999 two seniors at Columbine High School, Eric Harris and Dylan Klebold, went on a shooting spree that killed twelve students and a teacher at the Littleton, Colorado, school before killing themselves. Unfortunately, this was not an isolated incident. In the last few years, school shootings have occurred in such places as Pearl, Mississippi; Paducah, Kentucky; Jonesboro, Arkansas; Springfield, Oregon; and Santee, California. In many schools classmates bring chains, knives, and guns—and use them. In fact, violence has become so common in our public schools today that newspaper editors don't always think it is newsworthy enough to make the front page.

Researchers, however, are concerned. After interviewing nearly four thousand high school students from six public schools in Denver and Cleveland, sociologists are concluding that a substantial number of students are significantly traumatized by exposure to violence in the school systems. "We must consider exposure to violence a public health epidemic worthy of our most comprehensive and well-reasoned efforts," said the study from Case Western Reserve University in Cleveland. Anywhere from 33 to 43 percent of the male students said they had been slapped, hit, or punched at school. Three to 22 percent of the boys said they had been beaten or mugged in their neighborhoods. Also, from 3 to 33 percent of the male adolescents claim to have been shot or shot at within the previous year, and 6 to 16 percent said they been attacked or stabbed with a knife.

Among girls, 34 to 56 percent reported being slapped, hit, or punched at home. Up to 9 percent at one school said they had been attacked or stabbed with a knife, and up to 12 percent said they had been shot or shot at. The researchers hypothesized that the abnormal reading they were registering in the areas of anxiety, depression, anger, and stress among these young people was caused by this exposure to violence.[1]

Drug use in school is also commonplace. Nearly one million juveniles under the age of twenty are alcoholics. Some one hundred thousand ten- and eleven-year-olds get drunk at least once a week. One out of every twenty high school seniors smokes marijuana as well as consumes alcohol on a daily basis.

Young people face problems that their parents never did. You need to keep an open mind and open ears if you plan to teach them to deal with today's problems. The Bible still has the answers, but we need to be aware that our children and grandchildren are asking different questions than we did. Those questions are a lot tougher and call for the best possible teacher. That teacher is the man of the house.

Avoid irritability. We live in a high-stress world. With mergers, downsizing, and rapidly changing technology, job security is a thing of the past.

Stress produces irritability. Too often men take out their irritability on their family. This causes stress and irritability on their part. Perhaps you've seen the cartoon where the boss chews out the father. The father comes home and takes it out on his wife. The wife gets angry with the child. The child punishes the dog. And the dog chases the cat. What this doesn't show is the damage done to the relationships within this family. If this scenario happens frequently or on a long-term basis, any ability to teach spiritual truths is destroyed.

Avoid favoritism. Tom and Dick Smothers (The Smothers Brothers) made a fortune off the humor generated by Tom's accusation that their mother loved Dick best. In real life, favoritism isn't funny. This blunder leaves wounds that even time has difficulty healing. One couldn't help wonder if, underneath the humor, Tom didn't actually feel some of the pain he joked about.

Scripture chronicles a number of situations where favoritism was shown—all of them with disastrous results. Isaac was one of the Patriarchs, but his favoritism toward Esau and the corresponding favoritism of Jacob by Rebekah led to a vow of murder and a twenty-year separation between the twin brothers. Jacob also showed favoritism toward his son Joseph. That led to conspiracy, slave trading, and a cover-up.

Every instance of favoritism recorded in the Bible brought resentment and heartache into the home. To make matters worse, it also hindered the teaching of spiritual values.

Children are not assembly line products, each one exactly like the next. They differ in temperament and personality, so they can't be treated alike, but they do have to be treated as equals. The task of the father-teacher is to identify the differences in his children and maximize those differences in the way he teaches them.

A wise father is like friends of mine who live in Bethlehem, Israel. They are a family of woodcarvers who make some of the most beautiful olive wood carvings in the world. Before they begin to carve each one, the woodcarver studies the grain of the wood. He observes the bend of the raw material, and then he works with the natural qualities in the wood instead of against them. If he were to do otherwise, the wood eventually would crack under the stress.

In the same way, the man who wants to build a godly home needs to study his children. He needs to know their natural aptitudes and interests—not so he can favor one, or even compare one against the other, but so he can treat them all fairly and teach them equally about God and His will.

The Dos

Just as you can't win a baseball game with a good defense alone, you can't be an effective teacher by simply avoiding the don'ts. In addition to advice on how not to raise children, Ephesians 6:4 provides the following positive counsel on how to do the job right. Fathers are to "bring them up." The Greek word literally means to "nourish" them, to "cause them to grow." How are you to do that? Verse 4 says through "training" and "admonition."

The Greek word translated as "training" (*paideia*) occurs six times in the New King James Version. Three times it's translated "chastening," and once each as "nurture," "instruction," and "chastisement." It carries the idea of teaching through actively doing something together.

If a person wants to teach his child to fish, he doesn't merely hand him a book on fishing. Instead, he takes the youngster fishing. By the same token, if you want to teach your child about mercy, take him some place (perhaps a shelter or a mission) where you can participate together in acts of mercy.

The word *admonition*, on the other hand, implies verbal teaching. This is teaching in the traditional sense. It implies the imparting of knowledge.

Children are not being taught today. Many are ignorant of basic biblical facts—what I would call the "stuff of Scripture." Until our kids learn the stories, the characters, and the time lines, they will not have a framework on which to hang Bible doctrine later. In a survey of children, such gems of "knowledge" as these showed up:

- Noah's wife was Joan of Ark.
- When Mary heard she was to be the mother of Jesus, she went off and sang the Magna Carta.
- Holy acrimony is another name for marriage.
- The epistles are the wives of the apostles.
- Sodom and Gomorrah were husband and wife.

This may seem humorous, but it's also sad. If children don't know the facts taught in God's Word, how can they be expected to apply such principles as honesty, faithfulness, and compassion?

The biblical approach to teaching our children becomes apparent when you put these methods together—the training and the admonition. God would have the teacher in the home communicate truth through both actions and verbal instruction. The following suggestions have been helpful for my family:

Be available. The greatest ability we can bring to the task of teaching our children is availability. Often we're like the man who was engrossed in his evening paper. His son came into the room and asked, "Dad, who is God's wife?"

"Beats me, son," the father replied absentmindedly.

The boy was silent for a moment and then questioned, "Dad, why is the world round?"

Without putting his paper down, the man answered offhandedly, "I don't know, son."

The boy waited a brief time and then hesitantly inquired, "Dad, do you mind me asking all these questions?"

"Certainly not," his father replied from behind his paper. "How else are you going to learn anything?"

Children, especially young ones, have a million questions. The good news is that they are much more open to listening to answers to their questions than to lectures from their father. The bad news is that their questions seldom come at a convenient time.

Availability means setting aside the things you want to do and offering quality listening time. There is no sin in saying, "I don't know, but I'll find out." The sin is not being willing to listen in the first place.

Be simple. Stories abound of children who become confused because adults don't make themselves clear. One of my favorites is of the little girl who began her prayer, "Harold, please bless Mommy and Daddy."

"Wait a minute," her mother broke in. "Who is Harold?"

"Harold is God's name," the little girl replied.

"Who told you that?" her mother asked.

"I learned it at church," she said. "Don't you remember we prayed, 'Our Father, who art in heaven, Harold be Thy name'?"

Part of the genius of Jesus' teaching was His simplicity. Children flocked to His side to hear Him speak. They listened to Him because they could understand Him. The Savior used common things as He taught, such as sheep and shepherds, grain and sowers, fish and fishermen. Everyone understood what Jesus taught except when He used parables to deliberately hide the meaning.

When teaching children, use language appropriate for the age level. If you have to use a word that the child might be unfamiliar with, use another word along with it that will explain what it means. Also, don't assume because a child has heard such terms as *sanctification, Rapture, propitiation,* or even *salvation* all of his life that he understands them.

Be relevant. One little girl said to her mother, "Mommy, I wish I lived back in Bible times." "Why?" her mother asked. "Things seem so much more exciting in those days," she replied.

What a shame! If only that little girl and her mother knew that what's happening in our time is as exciting as the Bible times. There are more people alive today than have ever lived. That means there are more opportunities to share Christ than ever before. Revivals are occurring in many places around the world. People groups (people with a common language and culture) are being reached that have never heard the Gospel. Opportunities to give and serve and pray abound more today than at any other time in history.

To stay current, my family and I used Patrick Johnstone's *Operation World* every evening in our family devotions. In this book Dr. Johnstone teaches how to pray for the world country by country every day of your life. His late wife, Jill Johnstone, wrote *You Can Change the World*, the children's version of *Operation World*. It contains an alphabetical listing of twenty-six people groups and twenty-six countries—one section a week for the year.

Begin now to teach your children that God is real and active throughout the world. Teach them to see the world as He sees it. Help them to develop a heart like God's that longs to see the world come to know the Savior.

Be early. Often I hear parents say, "I don't want to teach my kids now. They're too young. I'll wait until they are older so they can make a choice." What these adults fail to realize is that a child does his best learning when he is young. Some child specialists say that 50 percent of a child's intellectual development occurs between birth and the age of four.

Young children are pliable. They can be molded and shaped; teenagers are less so. Allen Bean, one of my associates at Back to the Bible, related how his young daughter, Rachel, learned about pliability. She had received several cans of Play-Doh for her birthday. After spending a delightful afternoon molding and shaping a variety of objects out of the clay, it was time to clean up. She carefully put the clay back into the cans but didn't put the lids on. When she went back a few days later to play with it, the dough had become hard and unmoldable. Sometimes our children become the same way.

Ruth Graham, wife of evangelist Billy Graham, wrote, "The time for teaching and training is preteen. When they reach the teen years, it's time to shut up and listen."

If you feel you failed to teach your children, you can still reach out to your grandchildren. While their parents have the primary responsibility for them, don't downplay your role. *The Columbus Dispatch* quoted Art Linkletter, who at the age of eighty said that one of the greatest rewards for a senior citizen is "to pass on what he knows and spend time with his grandchildren, giving them a connection with the past."

As important as the past is, grandparents also can give their grandchildren a connection with the future. Numerous children credit their grandparents for leading them to Christ. Another associate of mine, Don Hawkins, told me that he led his six-year-old grandson, Albert, to the Lord while the boy was spending a week with his grandparents.

But don't wait too long to begin your teaching. While your children are still moldable, shape them to glorify God. It's sad to see parents neglect their children when they're young and then agonize over them when they are teens and adults. Scripture says, "Train up a child in the way he should go, and when he is old he will not depart from it" (Proverbs 22:6).

Be ready. Turn ordinary times into teaching occasions. As you play games, use them as opportunities to teach your children how to win and lose graciously. As you walk in the park or woods, plant your garden, or water your flowers, impress upon your children the wonder, beauty, and complexity of God's world. Emphasize the evidence that points to a Creator God rather than a random process of evolution.

Be patient. Worthwhile things seldom happen quickly. A young man approached the president of his Bible college and said, "Sir, I don't want to spend four years in the classroom. I want to be out preaching and saving souls. Is there some way I can shorten my course of study?"

"Well, son," the older man replied, "when God wants to grow a squash it takes months. When He wants to grow an oak tree it takes years. Which do you want to be?"

Teaching our children is a long-term contract. It's like putting money in a bank. A little bit on a regular basis adds up, but it takes a while.

Scripture says training takes place on a continuous basis: "For precept must be upon precept, precept upon precept, line upon line, line upon line, here a little, there a little" (Isaiah 28:10). Isaiah said this in a negative sense as he spoke to the people of Israel because they refused to listen to his teaching. But equally true, this is how we teach the truths of the Christian faith in the positive sense. We don't drop it all in one big chunk; we string it out. We look for those teachable moments when one more precept can be added to the precepts we've taught before.

Furthermore, don't assume once your children are grown that your teaching responsibilities are over. Learning is a lifetime experience, and teaching your children is a lifetime commitment. At the right moment, be ready to share with your adult children the wisdom God has taught you through the years.

THE WAY IT IS

The average American family is in a spiritual crisis. For the last several generations, fathers have failed to live up to their responsibility to be the teachers in their homes. The consequences have been unfortunate.

In 221 B.C. the Chinese were threatened by nomadic peoples from the north. To secure their borders they began building an enormous wall more than fifteen hundred miles long and ranging from fifteen- to thirty-feet thick at the base. The walls reached a height of twenty-five feet. It was finally finished during the Ming Dynasty (A.D. 1368–1644). The wall did its job well—only three times was it ever breached, and all three times the enemy bribed a gatekeeper to let them through.

The Chinese relied upon the material security of their wall. But they forgot that even the strongest security system can be breached if those who are responsible for it have not been taught what's right.

According to *The Washington Post*, Ronald Reagan made this observation, "If we fail to instruct our children in justice, religion, and liberty, we will be condemning them to a world without virtue, a life in the twilight of a civilization where the great truths have been forgotten."[2]

An alarming article in *The Wall Street Journal* labeled juvenile delinquency as a "growth business." Unfortunately, the description fits the situation. The article stated, "According to Youth Services, the arrest rate for murder by juveniles quadrupled in the past 25 years, and the rate for rape and robbery more than doubled. In dollars, the reform-school market amounts to more than $3 billion annually."[3] Could this indicate that we are near the "twilight of civilization"?

What the head of the home chooses to do obviously has a ripple effect that reaches far beyond the home. Bill Gothard, founder of Institute in Basic Life Principles, said, "We have weak churches today because we have weak families; we have weak families because we have weak husbands and fathers; we have weak husbands and fathers because they have not been taught basic scriptural principles."

It all comes back to the fathers. We need to reinstate the man of the house as the spiritual teacher of his home. You don't need a seminary degree. A good concordance, a Bible dictionary, a well-read Bible, and a willingness to devote time to the task could make all the difference for your family.

Touch the future. Teach your children.

[1] "Violence Impacting Youngsters' Minds," America Online, February 7, 1995.

[2] *The Washington Post*, August 24, 1984, p. A-7.

[3] John R. Dorfman, "King of Reform Schools Eyes Orphanages," *The Wall Street Journal*, February 1, 1995, p. B-1.

Chapter 4

THE PROTECTOR IN HIS HOME

Steven Greenberg woke early one fall morning and stumbled out of bed to answer a banging at the door of his Park Avenue penthouse. Two men on the other side identified themselves as police officers. They said they had a search warrant and ordered him to open the door. He did.

Once inside, the men put a gun to his head and growled, "This is a robbery!" Helpless, Mr. Greenberg watched as the counterfeit officers carried away art deco antiques valued at $250,000. Fortunately, they spared his life.

The New York City Police Department claims it receives an average of thirteen hundred police impersonation complaints each year. The department speculates the true number is actually higher because many go unreported. These false policemen commit everything from robbery to murder while under the guise of keeping the law.

These are violent days. No major war engulfs our world, but violence is threatening our streets and homes. On any given day, many dangers knock at our door. Some are physical; they pose danger to our well-being and safety. Others are spiritual; they jeopardize our growing conformity to Christ. Still others are moral; they are a threat to the maintenance of order in society. But whatever the source of danger, God still holds the man of the house responsible to protect his home against such hazards.

Jesus understood these dangers. He was the object of many attacks, especially by a group of religious leaders called the Pharisees. They continually sought opportunities to discredit Him and mislead the people.

On one occasion Jesus walked through a grainfield on the Sabbath day. His disciples were hungry, so they innocently picked some grain to eat. The Pharisees were infuriated. If Jesus were a rabbi, how could He allow His followers to break the Law like that? Jesus replied, "Have you not read what David did when he was hungry, he and those who were with him: how he entered the house of God and ate the showbread which was not lawful for him to eat, nor for those who were with him, but only for the priests? . . . The Son of Man is Lord even of the Sabbath" (Matthew 12:3–4, 8). Although they refused to acknowledge it, the Pharisees were talking to One greater than the Law. He was the Lord of the Sabbath, not the servant of it. He spoke the truth, but that grieved the religious leaders all the more.

On another occasion a sightless deaf man was brought to Jesus. This double infirmity was bad enough, but the man was also demon-possessed. Jesus healed him and cast out the demons (Matthew 12:22).

The people were amazed; the Pharisees were enraged. They accused Jesus of casting out demons by the power of Satan. How absurd! Jesus could not allow this charge to pass without a challenge, and in the process, He asked one of the most engaging questions in the Bible: "How can one enter a strong man's house and plunder his goods, unless he first binds the strong man?" (Matthew 12:29).

Jesus reasoned that it was ridiculous to think that He cast out demons in the power of Satan, for demons are Satan's minions. They do the devil's bidding. Why would the devil invoke his power to cast his own followers out of the unfortunate man? It didn't make sense. As Jesus pointed out, "Every kingdom divided against itself is brought to desolation, and every city or house divided against itself will not stand" (Matthew 12:25).

But the question Jesus asked is much more instructive than showing the absurdity of the Pharisees' charge. It teaches us one of the basic lessons of life. You cannot plunder a man's home until you first bind the strong man. Satan cannot enter a man's house and plunder his wife and family until he first neutralizes the husband in the home. The key to keeping Satan outside of the home is the man.

Our homes are only as strong as our men. When a man leaves a home or will not accept his responsibility in the home, the ability of the wife to keep Satan outside the door is severely weakened.

In this rapidly destabilizing world, the man who wants to build a godly home must stand between the dangers at the door and his family in the house. We must have a good grasp of what we are up against. After all, that next knock at the door may not be a friend.

PHYSICAL DANGERS

When anyone mentions danger at our door, physical dangers immediately come to mind. And why not? These dangers are very real.

Street crime

Crime on the street takes a daily toll in our cities. Many years ago my family and I were visiting the Statue of Liberty in New York Harbor. I didn't want to pay what I thought were exorbitant fees to park in an off-street lot, so I parked my van on the street at a meter. It was in plain sight of hundreds of people who passed it every few minutes.

After our visit to Lady Liberty we returned to our van. One of my daughters ran ahead, opened the door, and got into the van. *How did she do that?* I thought. *I locked the van.* Sure enough, it had been broken into, and every auto parked at a meter on that street suffered the same fate.

What was most amazing to me, however, was what I learned when I called the police to report the theft. It was mid-afternoon, and the officer I spoke to assigned a case number to me. It was 1296. My curiosity got the best of me. "Officer, does that mean you have had 1,295 thefts reported already today?" To my surprise he said, "That's what it means."

Gang violence

Another major cause of crime is gang activity. What used to be a problem only in our large cities is rapidly beginning to plague small towns and rural villages. One Asian gang that operated crime rings from Florida to California had its headquarters in a small Pennsylvania town with a population of less than forty-five hundred.

We may disagree with many of the policies implemented by Jocelyn Elders when she served for a time as surgeon general under President Bill Clinton. But she gave us reason to stop and ponder when she told a House Government Operations Committee, "For too many young people, it's easier to find a gun than a good friend, a good teacher, or a good school." The man who wants to build a godly home must know what is going on in his community; more than that, he needs to work with law enforcement and community leaders to protect his home.

Scams

Scam artists also continue to flourish. A few years ago, a con man was arrested for pulling scams in the Midwest. When police checked his record, they received a printed rap sheet more than eight feet long. The man had used twenty-two known aliases, nine birthdates, and eight Social Security numbers. In a crime spree that stretched from Denver, Colorado, to Omaha, Nebraska, he had bilked various companies of merchandise valued between $300,000 to $500,000.[1]

Often, however, scam artists prey on the elderly by persuading them to invest their life savings in some scheme that is as solid as the fizz from a can of pop. Dorothy Korten of Omaha was one of those victims. The seventy-one-year-old woman was persuaded to take $12,800 out of her bank account and give it to a man posing as a "bank official." This man claimed someone was looting her account and they needed the money to catch the culprit. Too late, Ms. Korten discovered that the real thief was the man to whom she gave the money.

The telephone is another tool frequently used to steal from people. It has given many unscrupulous individuals direct access to our homes. While there are many legitimate companies that use the telephone for marketing, consumers lose an estimated $40 billion a year through telemarketing fraud. A Louis Harris Survey conducted for the National Consumers League found that 92 percent of adults in the United States reported receiving fraudulent telephone offers. And the FBI estimates that there are fourteen thousand illegal telephone sales operations bilking consumers in the United States every day.[2]

Don't be surprised if someone shows up on your doorstep with a once-in-a-lifetime offer on siding, paint jobs, or a hundred other products or services. Every year somebody comes to my house with a load of firewood for sale, claiming it was cut a season ago and has aged more than a year. Each time I inspect the wood, it's as green as if it were cut last week. It probably was.

We all acknowledge these physical dangers. They make the headlines in our newspapers and the lead stories on the evening news. No one questions that we need to protect ourselves from their harm. But what may be the more deadly dangers are often overlooked. They are the spiritual and moral dangers that bang on our door and intrude into our lives. Yet these are just as real as the physical dangers.

SPIRITUAL DANGERS

In the 1950s and 1960s, Americans and the Western world in general believed science could solve all of man's problems. If science didn't have the answer now, it would find one in the near future. Science became a god to many in the industrialized world.

But beginning in the 1970s a sense of disillusionment gradually set in. The Vietnam War proved that science couldn't provide world peace. The resurgence of antibiotic-resistant bacteria shook the confidence of those looking for a disease-free future.

Tim Stevens wrote in *Industry Week*, "There is an increasing decline of faith in rationality and the scientific approach. We are coming to the pessimistic conclusion that science can't prove everything and can't solve all our problems, even if we did send a man to the moon."[3]

People have become conscious of a general feeling of emptiness and lack of purpose. As a consequence, they are looking for something on which to pin their hopes. Often they look in the wrong places.

The occult

Spiritism, fortune-telling, and seances are a growing menace to our homes. Every major newspaper in the United States carries a column on astrology. There are at least twelve million people in the United States (including one former first lady) who believe that their lives can be influenced by the arrangement of the stars and planets. One source estimates that Americans keep 175,000 part-time and 10,000 full-time astrologers busy.

Many people followed Jeanne Dixon and heralded her as a "messenger from God." Yet in a *Christianity Today* article, David Myers points out:

Not only did Jeanne Dixon never predict anything so precise as, "John Kennedy will be elected, but then assassinated," she also changed her mind before his election and said that Richard Nixon would be elected in 1960. Other predictions included that Pope Paul would enjoy a year of good health (he died), that the Panama Canal Treaty would be defeated in Congress (it was approved), Marie Osmond would not marry (two months later she did), and that Ted Kennedy would be elected President in 1980 (wrong again!).[4]

It's a good thing for Ms. Dixon that she didn't live during the days of the Old Testament. Any one of those failed predictions would have brought her a death by stoning. God says, "But the prophet who presumes to speak a word in My name, which I have not commanded him to speak, or who speaks in the name of other gods, that prophet shall die.

. . . when a prophet speaks in the name of the LORD, if the thing does not happen or come to pass, that is the thing which the LORD has not spoken; the prophet has spoken it presumptuously; you shall not be afraid of him" (Deuteronomy 18:20–22).

Today's clairvoyants and psychics talk about their percentage of correct predictions. But that wouldn't do for God's prophets. They had to be right 100 percent of the time or there was no future left for them to predict. That's how someone could tell if a prophet was from God.

Nasty novelties

But other spiritual dangers come knocking at our door. Ouija boards, crystal balls, and Tarot cards are among the fastest-selling novelties in many large department stores. They are the favorite of a lot of teens and have one thing in common: they are objects designed to seek knowledge apart from God. More than one teenager has "divined" something weird from an Ouija board and ruined a life.

The Bible takes these spiritual dangers seriously. In Deuteronomy 18:10–11 God declares, "There shall not be found among you anyone who . . . practices witchcraft, or a soothsayer, or one who interprets omens, or a sorcerer, or one who conjures spells, or a medium, or a spiritist, or one who calls up the dead."

Maybe you think God is trying to monopolize the information superhighway. Perhaps you feel God has declared, "If you're going to know anything, you're going to have to learn it directly from Me." But that's not true. God does not need Ouija boards or crystal balls to impart wisdom and knowledge to us; that's why we have a Bible.

The Bible is our source for knowing the mind of God, not cards and trinkets and visions. The source for those occult tools is Satan. He is a crafty person, but he is not omniscient as God is. Only God knows the future entirely. Only He can be trusted to reveal it to us. When we allow other so-called sources of wisdom in our homes, we're opening the door to danger.

Just because Satan is not omniscient does not mean he is stupid. After all, he has lived longer than the total existence of the human race. He must have learned something during that time. Plus, he has innumerable fallen angels to feed information to him.

But you can't trust anything Satan tells you. He is the great deceiver. Jesus said Satan is a liar and the father of lies (John 8:44). He uses whatever knowledge he has to his own advantage. He tells you enough to lure you in and make you feel comfortable, but then he springs the trap. Satan's goal is to destroy you, not inform you.

Someone once said, "If people's craving for the mysterious, the wonderful, the supernatural is not fed on true religion, it will feed itself on the garbage of any superstition that is offered."[5] All too often this happens with our children because Satan was allowed to enter the house while the strong man was bound.

Two by two

Equally threatening are the cults. Like the occult, they take advantage of people's spiritual hunger. And they are growing at light-year speed.

In 1963, Anthony Hoekema of Calvin Seminary covered the most important cults fairly well in a book entitled *The Four Major Cults*. In the almost forty years since, cults have proliferated to the point that, according to J. Gordon Melton, author of *Encyclopedic Handbook of Cults in America*, there are at least seven hundred cults active in the United States. Most of these are small and limited in influence. Others, such as the Mormons and Jehovah's Witnesses, are firmly established, well financed, and aggressively evangelizing in your neighborhood and all over the world.

The man who wants to build a godly home has the responsibility as the spiritually strong man to make sure these people do not come into his home and poison his family. This is just as important—maybe more important—than protecting his loved ones from physical danger. If the man of the house is bound spiritually, it is easy for Satan to enter the house and plunder the family.

The lunatic fringe

Fringe cults, as opposed to some of the better-known cults, can be life-threatening to your family. That might be considered an overstatement had it not been for men like Jim Jones, David Koresh, Luc Jouret, or Marshall Applewhite.

Some nine hundred followers of self-proclaimed messiah Jim Jones committed suicide in Jonestown, Guyana, in 1978. Many of them were families who were unprotected by the strong man. In April 1993 David Koresh, leader of the Branch Davidians, died along with seventy of his followers in a fiery apocalypse in a commune near Waco, Texas. Where was the strong man of those families? Luc Jouret, a Zairian-born physician and spiritual explorer, led fifty-three of his followers to death in October 1994 in a mass death/suicide pact. Marshall Applewhite convinced thirty-eight of his followers to kill themselves in March 1997 with the promise that they would be transported to a UFO trailing the Hale-Bopp comet. When the husband in the home is bound, the lunatics at the door are free to plunder and kill.

There is a stern warning in 1 John 4:1: "Do not believe every spirit, but test the spirits to see whether they are from God, because many false prophets have gone out into the world." When these false prophets knock on your door with their books and magazines, it's your job as the protector in the home to make sure none of their propaganda gets across the threshold. When they solicit your young teenagers, you must expose them for what they are.

That is what the apostle Paul was thinking about when he wrote, "For I know this, that after my departure savage wolves will come in among you, not sparing the flock. . . . Therefore watch, and remember that for three years I did not cease to warn everyone night and day with tears" (Acts 20:29, 31).

MORAL DANGERS

But not all the dangers come so openly to our door. When Satan cannot destroy the family from the outside, he works from within.

Military tacticians have known this ploy for centuries. During the Spanish Civil War, the rebel General Mola surrounded the city of Madrid. Someone asked the general which of his four columns would be the first to enter the besieged town. "The fifth," he replied. The questioner looked confused. Smiling, the general explained, "You forget my sympathizers who are already in the city!"

Although none of us ever deliberately sets out to be Satan's tools, it does happen. Through Satan's trickery or through our own carelessness, the devil has ways of winning supporters even from within our home.

Talking out the garbage

One tactic Satan uses is to fill our homes with verbal garbage. He seeks to influence the subject matter of our conversations. The topics we discuss openly around the dinner table or in our living room need to be monitored and carefully governed by the strong man of the house. Ephesians 5:4 tells us, "Nor should there be obscenity, foolish talk or coarse joking, which are out of place, but rather thanksgiving."

The apostle Paul is not suggesting there be no levity in our homes. Nothing is more infectious than family laughter. Jesus Himself used humor to make His point. He talked about straining out gnats and swallowing camels, or plucking out a speck in someone's eye while encumbered with a log in our own. Surely these humorous extremes must have brought a smile from His listeners.

In recent years, however, much of the humor used by comedians is tasteless—but certainly not colorless or odorless. The late Steve Allen told a group of hospital staffers in Grand Rapids, Michigan, "It wouldn't have occurred to actors and comedians in the fifties to be so objectionable. American humor has never been as filthy as it is now."

Today it seems any topic, no matter how perverted or obscene, can be shared openly and without shame. But if the man of the house follows biblical standards, there will be some subjects discussed around the table, others discussed only in private, and still others that are not discussed at all. It is the job of the protector in the home to decide what falls into which category.

The innuendo, the off-colored joke, the smutty story—all need the attention of the strong man. Dad should set the example and then see to it that those he is charged to protect follow his example. If you make people wipe their feet before they come into your home, why not insist they "wipe" their minds and their mouths as well?

TV addiction

Television also is a potent influence on our lives. Many family members are addicted to this collection of plastic and microcircuits without even knowing it.

Good Housekeeping magazine reported an experiment run by a Detroit newspaper. The newspaper offered 120 families $500 if they would agree not to watch television for a month. Remarkably, only 27 families were even willing to try.

Five of these families were selected for the report. Each family had been watching between forty to seventy hours of TV a week (between 5.7 and 10 hours a day). The sudden removal of this stimulus actually created withdrawal symptoms for some. After the initial trauma, however, the participants experienced many good effects: families started to talk to one another more; they dug games out of storage and played; they pulled books off the shelf and read. The beneficial effects of kicking the habit were both remarkable and dramatic.

Unfortunately, once the month was over, the families all chose to resume their addictive habit of watching TV for nearly the same number of hours as before. Some even reported an increase in the time spent tied to the tube.

This makes you wonder if Paul's admonition in 1 Corinthians 6:12 should be applied to television. He said, "All things are lawful for me, but all things are not helpful. All things are lawful for me, but I will not be brought under the power of any." If television has that kind of control in your life, maybe it's time to break the bondage.

Time waster

In a speech on "The Trouble with Television," Robert MacNeil (formerly of the "MacNeil-Lehrer News Hour" on PBS) pointed out that TV is also a great time waster. We need opportunities to relax and "veg out," but those occasions must always be kept in balance with more constructive pursuits. Mr. MacNeil said,

> It's difficult to escape the influence of television. If you fit the statistical averages, by the age of twenty you will have been exposed to at least twenty thousand hours of television. You can add ten thousand hours for each decade you have lived after the age of twenty. The only things Americans do more than watch television are work and sleep.

> Calculate for a moment what could be done with even a part of those hours. Five thousand hours, I am told, are what a typical college undergraduate spends working on a bachelor's degree. In ten thousand hours you could have learned enough to become an astronomer or engineer. You could have learned several languages fluently. If it appealed to you, you could be reading Homer in the original Greek or Dostoyevsky in Russian. If it didn't, you could have walked around the world and written a book about it.

Every time I encourage Christians to have a personal quiet time with the Lord and family devotions daily, I receive letters from well-meaning folks who say, "You don't understand. I just don't have time to read the Bible and pray every day." I suggest they either consciously plan their TV viewing at the beginning of each week or just pull the plug altogether, and they will find a whole world of time that they never knew existed.

Mind shaper

Yet it's not just the addictive, time-wasting nature of television that should concern the man of the house. TV is highly influential in shaping the family's view of the world as well.

When the *National Enquirer* did a five-state survey, it found that most of the people polled could identify the TV character Bart Simpson but not their congressman. In fact, one respondent thought Bart Simpson was his congressman.

Many children find their role models in Saturday morning cartoon characters. Back in the days when the Power Rangers were the "in" cartoon characters, *The Wall Street Journal* reported that children as young as three years old were demonstrating an obsession with the martial arts antics of these futuristic superheroes. Fannie Elliott, a teacher at Kedren Headstart Preschool in Los Angeles, complained, "One simply has to say 'Trini' [a Power Ranger's name] and abracadabra, the little curmudgeons transform before my very eyes into an entire martial-arts army. First comes grunts and groans, then cries of 'Hi-Yah!' as the children's eyes take on a bewitched glint. Soon the classroom erupts into a Bruce Lee festival."[6]

Such problems have led a number of schools to ban all martial arts activity while on school property. Yet if we wonder where our children get their secular view of life, perhaps we should look no further than our living room. This is a job for the strong man, not the Power Rangers. It's time Dad became the kids' hero again.

Mind polluter

Furthermore, there is the pollution factor—not environmental pollution but mind pollution. When *TV Guide* asked its readers a few years ago if television was going too far, more than twenty thousand phone calls poured in. Ninety percent said that TV was definitely too permissive.

Even children are saying that TV goes too far. Young people responded to a nationwide survey saying that television encouraged them to take part in sexual activity too soon, to show disrespect for their parents, to lie, and to engage in aggressive behavior. Seventy-seven percent of those questioned said television shows too much pre-marital sex. Two-thirds claimed that programs like "The Simpsons" and "Married . . . With Children" encouraged them to act disrespectfully toward their parents.[7]

The liberal, permissive nature of the television industry comes as no surprise to those who know the people behind the programs. *Newsweek* magazine polled 104 top television writers and executives and found the following attitudes differ significantly from the rest of the nation:

Believe adultery is wrong

Hollywood 49%

Everyone else 85%

Have no religious affiliation

Hollywood 45%

Everyone else 4%

Believe homosexual acts are wrong

Hollywood 20%

Everyone else 76%

Believe in a woman's right to an abortion

Hollywood 97%

Everyone else 59%

Now we know why television is such a barren wasteland!

Unfortunately, this small group of liberals has an inordinate influence, especially on our young people. One study found that teenagers hear about or watch sexual activity on television two to three times an hour. With four to five hours of TV viewing a day, they accumulate at least three dozen instances or references to sexual behavior a week, or more than fifteen hundred acts or references each year. The study concluded that exposure to this onslaught of moral pollution may be a contributing factor to increased and earlier sexual activity on the part of teenagers.

Whether we are a teenager or an adult, the more we see of the filth on TV, the less sensitive we become to its true nature. The average American has become nearly shock-proof. Sadly, this destroys one of the defense mechanisms God built in to protect us from sin. New Zealand theologian E. M. Blaiklock said, "Our greatest security against sin is to be shocked by it." Could it be that we Christians have lost that security?

It falls on the shoulders of the protector in the home to know where the "off" button for this mind polluter is located and to use it often. If it can't be controlled, it should be removed.

Techno trash

Another recent moral polluter is the Internet. Twenty years ago, explicit, deviant, or violent pornography was confined to "adult" bookstores and theaters. In order to view such trash, it was necessary to risk public recognition and possible embarrassment. Now it is available privately on the Internet. A study conducted by Carnegie Mellon University found more than nine hundred thousand sexually explicit sites readily accessible on the World Wide Web.[8] With an increasing number of home computers connected to the Internet (one source indicated that 52 percent of the population, or about 144 million people in the United States, could surf the Web from home[9]), it is no surprise that a rising number of adults and children are falling victim to techno trash. In August 2000, nearly twenty-one million home Internet users logged on to pornographic sites.[10]

With the advent of affordable technology, the information superhighway is running right to our homes, down our halls, and into the rooms of our minds. Unless you want to risk your family becoming road kill, you must exercise your authority over the material to which your family is exposed.

Elizabeth Thoman, director for the Center for Media Literacy in Los Angeles and founding editor of *Media & Values* magazine, told a group of Christian leaders that parents must understand "that managing media in the home is now part of what it means to be a parent." That's just another way of saying that the protector in the home must be alert to the many ways in which the media can plunder his family.

Role muddles

Yet another danger inside the house is the immorality encouraged by movie role models. Describing one film he recently had seen, one critic wrote, "The plot moves rapidly down the sewer." That analysis could be applied to many other contributions by the motion picture industry. Another critic, E. O'Brien, writes, "If you're not an adult when you go in to see a movie these days, you sure are when you come out."

It should sober us when we consider the observation of Philip Myers in his book *Rome, Its Rise and Fall*. He wrote,

Almost from the beginning, the Roman stage was gross, and immorality was one of the main agencies to which must be attributed the undermining of the originally sound moral life of Roman society.

So absorbed did the people become in the indecent representations of the stage that they lost all thought and care of the affairs of real life.[11]

Today we have traded live actors for celluloid, but the outcome could well be the same.

Yet simply boycotting the movie theater is not the answer. Within months, any movie that can be seen at the theater can be rented at your local grocery store and played in your living room.

The Barna Research Group found that of the twenty-eight million households in the United States headed by born-again Christians, about twelve million own a VCR. In fact, Christian homes are as likely to have a VCR as non-Christian homes. Like fire, these instruments can be a blessing or a bane. A great deal of information and entertainment is accessible through video; however, much that is detrimental and degrading is also available.

The average North American household spends more than $100 each year on video rentals. One video store owner reported that it was not unusual for a father to rent a children's video for his kids and a couple of others with an adult theme for himself. Is this the role of the strong man? Ephesians 5:3 says, "But among you there must not be even a hint of sexual immorality, or any kind of impurity."

ETERNAL VIGILANCE

Being the protector is a big job, regardless of how strong the strong man is. The attacks of Satan are too frequent, too subtle, and too powerful. Thomas Jefferson reportedly said, "Eternal vigilance is the price of liberty." That's true in government; it's true in the family as well.

If you are the protector of your home, vigilance against those who would plunder your family is not an option; it's an imperative. Ask the Spirit of God to help you. Ask Him to give you discernment and wisdom beyond your years to judge what is harmful and what is helpful for your family. Be strong enough to hold the door shut when Satan knocks. Be strong enough to work out TV and video viewing guidelines by which you would be comfortable inviting Jesus Himself to sit and watch with your family.

In June 1989, a nineteen-year-old German named Mathias Rust flew a Cessna 172 airplane more than four hundred miles into Soviet airspace. He concluded his trip by landing in Moscow's Red Square near the Kremlin. In the ensuing furor, Soviet officials learned that their radar had spotted the plane in more than enough time to stop it, but those responsible for protecting Moscow assumed it was one of their own and no one attempted to identify it. Soviet air force jets even circled the small craft twice, but the investigation concluded the pilots showed "intolerable unconcern and indecision about cutting short the flight of the violator plane."

You and I are not unlike those Soviet defenders. We also have an enemy attempting to invade our space, our homes. This is not a time for indecision or tolerance. Satan is unquestionably out to destroy your family. He brings to your door and over your threshold every peril possible. He attacks on the physical front, the spiritual front, and the moral front. His attacks are simultaneous and relentless. If he can't plunder your family one way, he'll try another.

If you are the man of your house, pray for yourself. Pray for wisdom; pray for strength; pray for courage. Only with God's help can you protect your home, but that help is just a prayer away. If you love the man of your house, pray for him, support him, and encourage him.

The strong man is the protector in the home who stands between his wife and children and the attacks of Satan. If Satan can bind this person, you might as well hand him the key to the front door. But with God's help you can protect your home. He can keep you strong and unfettered. He can keep you vigilant and able to do battle.

One important factor in this process is worship. We explore the what, where, and how of strength-giving worship in the next chapter.

[1] Bruce Weible, "Professional Con Artist's Luck Runs Out," *The Lincoln Star*, February 14, 1995, pp. 1, 6.

[2] National Fraud Information Center
(http://www.fraud.org/telemarketing/teleset.htm).

[3] Tim Stevens, "Que Sera?," *Industry Week*, January 9, 1995, p. 48.

[4] David G. Myers, "ESP and the Paranormal," *Christianity Today*, July 15, 1983, p. 15.

[5] Myers, p. 16.

[6] Joseph Pereira, "Caution: 'Morphing' May Be Hazardous to Your Teacher," *The Wall Street Journal*, December 7, 1994, p. 1.

[7] "Children Say They Ape TV," *The Lincoln Star*, February 27, 1995, pp. 1, 6.

[8] Barbara Franceski, "Cyberporn: Is It Free Speech?" (http://cwfa.org/library/pornography/1998-05-15_internet.shtml).

[9] Jamie G. Kent, "The State of the Web—2000" (http://sidereal-designs.com/tlink/aug00.html~Out).

[10] Catherina Hurlburt, "Is Porn Here to Stay?" (http://cwfa.org/library/pornography/2000-10-20_stay.shtml).

[11] Philip Myers, *Rome, Its Rise and Fall* (Boston: Ginn, 1903), p. 123.

Chapter 5

THE WORSHIPER IN HIS HOME

Bob Dylan was right: "The times, they are a-changin'."

This is especially true of worship. If you haven't been to church lately, be warned. Worship services have changed so dramatically you might not recognize them.

In some churches, praise is in and worship is out. Choruses are in; hymns are out. Feelings are in; facts are out. Melody is in; message is out. Happy is in; holy is out.

Not that these are wrong. Praising God is great. Happiness in the Lord is wonderful. A striking melody is fine. But when one good thing excludes another, you always lose. In some churches, real worship is becoming scarce.

Throw into the mix the differences between the generations—the G. I. Generation, the Baby Boomers, Generation X (also known as the Busters or the Xers)—and the approach you take to worship in your church requires using kid gloves. And what's difficult to agree upon in church is doubly trying in the intimacy of the home. It's a challenge these days for a man to lead his family in worship.

WHAT IS WORSHIP?

Maybe we could accommodate more diversity if we could agree on what worship is. If we understand what it means to worship God, perhaps we can come to enjoy the variety of expressions worship may take.

Worship comes from the Anglo-Saxon word *weorthscipe*. Eventually this word developed into *worship*, a combination of *worth*, meaning "value" or "significance," and *ship*, meaning "full of." Common people used it as a term of address for those they considered their superiors, like we use *sir* today.

Occasionally the word *worship* is still used as a title of honor. I once represented Lincoln, Nebraska, to the mayor of Lincoln, England. Before meeting with him in the seven-hundred-year-old town guildhall, I was briefed on protocol. While I was instructed to refer to him simply as "Mr. Mayor," I noticed the certificate he presented to me gave his title as "His Worship the Mayor."

When we worship God, we come to One who is our superior with the intent of expressing how full of value and worth we find Him. Every generation should be able to agree upon this.

Worship is inherent to man. In fact, the Greek word for "man" (*anthropos*) means "the up-looking one." Archaeologists have found indications that even the earliest civilizations engaged in some form of worship. We shouldn't be surprised; the apostle Paul says, "For since the creation of the world His invisible attributes are clearly seen, being understood by the things that are made, even His eternal power and Godhead, so that they are without excuse" (Romans 1:20).

There are no people groups known today that do not worship something. All of us possess a natural inclination for worship, although not everyone expresses it the same way or toward the same object. Even an atheist, who claims to have no god, holds man in reverence and awe. He worships himself instead of God.

We can't help but worship. Yet many people do not understand the importance of it.

WHY WORSHIP GOD?

True worship sincerely expresses to God how meaningful and precious He is. But why is it important that you, as a man, take up the responsibility of worship leader in your home? What do you get out of worshiping God? What does your family gain from your leadership in worship? More significant, why does God think it's important? Let's explore some answers.

From God's perspective

Let's begin with a divine view of worship. From God's perspective, why is our worship important? Why is it necessary?

God is worthy

When the Greeks and Romans created their gods, they made them like themselves. Their gods committed adultery, incest, and murder. They were drunkards and carousers. They were no better than the ones who worshiped them—only more powerful.

Manmade gods are usually like that—reflections of their creators. There is an unusual place in Kyoto, Japan, called "The Temple of the Thousand Buddhas." Inside are one thousand shrines, each containing a figure of Buddha that is slightly different from the others. They are there so the worshiper can enter, find one that looks the most like himself, and worship it.

This stands in stark contrast to Jehovah. Our God is worthy of our worship because He is so unlike us. We are dirty and soiled; God is pure and holy. We are selfish and self-centered; God is compassionate and loving. No one is more worthy of our worship.

Thus, the man of the house worships God because He is worthy of it. Revelation 4:11 reminds us, "You are worthy, O Lord, to receive glory and honor and power; for You created all things, and by Your will they exist and were created."

At the end of John's great revelation of heaven and the future, he says, "Now I, John, saw and heard these things. And when I heard and saw, I fell down to worship before the feet of the angel who showed me these things. Then he said to me, 'See that you do not do that. For I am your fellow servant, and of your brethren the prophets, and of those who keep the words of this book. Worship God'" (Revelation 22:8–9).

The command is plain, simple, and straight from an angel's mouth. Worship God. No part of creation, not even the angels, qualify to receive the honor and glory due to the Lord. God alone is worthy.

God wants our worship

We worship God because He wants it. In fact, God commands it, and He is justifiably eager to receive it.

God called Moses to the holy mountain to worship Him (Exodus 24:1). He forbade the worship of any other gods (34:14) and issued stern warnings against those who did (Deuteronomy 30:15–20). Many of the psalms encourage the worship of God (Psalm 29:2; 95:6).

Jesus told the woman at the well, "But the hour is coming, and now is, when the true worshippers will worship the Father in spirit and truth; for the Father is seeking such to worship Him" (John 4:23). This is the only place in the Bible where we are told that God seeks anything from us. He seeks our sincere and genuine worship.

If you are desiring to build a godly home, take special note. God doesn't want foremost your works or your wealth; He wants your worship. And He seeks you to lead your family in worship.

From man's perspective

Having seen God's view of the appropriateness and necessity of worship, let's now turn to man's perspective. Why should we worship God? What are the benefits to us?

We need to sharpen our skills

In Revelation 4, the apostle John reveals what heavenly worship will be like. He says, "Whenever the living creatures give glory and honor and thanks to Him who sits on the throne, who lives forever and ever, the twenty-four elders fall down before Him who sits on the throne and worship Him who lives forever and ever, and cast their crowns before the throne" (vv. 9–10).

As John sees it, heaven is one big worship celebration. Since that's true, then it's important for us to sharpen our worship skills now. Your home is like a practice field for heaven. You have watched all the training films and read all the playbooks. Now it's time for a worship scrimmage. It's your opportunity to lead your family in an activity that has eternal significance. You have the privilege as the man of the house to model worship and to teach it to others.

To view it another way, life could be considered an entry-level worship class—Worship 101. In the throes of life's trials and joys you learn to lift your heart and lips in worship to God. You won't always do it the right way down here, but when life is over and "school is out," when you enter God's eternal home, you will worship Him as you have never done before.

But it begins here and now. This is the time you start learning to worship the Lord in spirit and in truth.

We need to express our love

If the prospect of a glorious, continuous worship service in heaven doesn't excite you, if you fear it will be boring, you've forgotten the love factor. Love is what makes worship exciting. Worship is the primary way we express our love for God.

Do you remember when you first fell in love? Remember how you could hardly wait to see that special person again? The hours at school or work dragged on until the moment you were once again in the presence of your loved one. None of this was boring to you, was it? Absolutely not! It was the most exciting time in your life. Just being together made the hours fly. There weren't enough hours in the day to satisfy your desire to be with her.

If you take those feelings and magnify them a hundredfold or more, you get some idea of what heaven will be like. J. Oswald Sanders says, "There can be no worship where there is no love. The prime requirement of the law was 'Thou shalt love the Lord thy God with all thy heart, and with all thy soul, and with all thy might' (Deuteronomy 6:5)."[1]

Heaven will be filled with both unimaginable love and overflowing worship. For the first time in your life, you will know what it is like to be loved unconditionally and accepted unreservedly. As a consequence, you will be motivated to respond in kind with worship. It won't be a chore. It won't be a burden. More than anything else, you will want to worship.

We need to regain our perspective

Worship also puts life back into focus again. Men tend to hold their frustrations inside until they explode. We ponder our hurts until they become the central point of our lives. We cogitate until we agitate. When that happens, we grow bitter and disappointed.

Worship realigns the center of our lives. Instead of dwelling on the negatives of life, worship causes us to concentrate on the positives of God. Rather than enumerating our problems, worship leads us to count our blessings. We realize anew that no matter how big our difficulties may be, God is bigger still.

In addition, worship reminds us who is in charge. The issue of control is a constant battle in the Christian life. The man of the house typically falls into the trap of thinking he can run his life (and maybe the lives of those around him). Invariably, his attempts end in a flop.

The control issue is often the hidden agenda behind those who deny that God exists. Aldous Huxley, an outspoken atheist and brother to Thomas Huxley, the famous evolutionist, late in his life openly admitted that his dislike for the Scriptures and his derogatory attacks on the Christian faith stemmed from his desire for the freedom to sin. He wrote, "I had motives for not wanting the world to have a meaning. Consequently assuming that it had none, I was able without any difficulty to find satisfying reasons for this assumption. . . . For myself, the philosophy of meaninglessness was essentially an instrument of liberation, sexual and political."

By his own admission, Huxley rejected Christianity and embraced evolution because he didn't want to be responsible to God. He wanted to be in charge, to run his life as he saw fit. Aldous Huxley lived by that philosophy and was miserable the whole time.

We need the accountability

Accountability is an idea whose time has come. To be accountable means you can furnish justifiable reasons for your actions; you are able to provide an explanatory analysis of who you are and what you do. It's simply a matter of being responsible.

The man who seeks to build a godly home needs accountability. Any husband who is not accountable will be prone to treat his wife as a servant and his children as unwanted nuisances. This fosters a home with no spiritual base, no spiritual leadership, and no spiritual direction. It also can lead to domestic violence and child abuse.

Bob Greene of the *Chicago Tribune* knows about accountability. He has a theory about what's wrong with the world. He blames it on what he calls the "Death of the Permanent Record."

You might remember that if you misbehaved in grade school, it was noted on your "permanent record." That threat caused most of us to think twice before we did something deceitful or unethical. We didn't hesitate because we were good little cherubs; we hesitated for fear of having our actions written on our permanent record.

Greene suggests that today people have concluded that there is no such thing as a permanent record. In fact, they believe no one has a right to keep track. He says that with today's emphasis on our right to privacy, if a schoolchild ever was threatened with something going on his permanent record, he would probably file suit under the Freedom of Information Act and get his hands on his files before recess.

But through worship, both at church and in the family, men are reminded that there is still someone keeping record. We might sneak around and fool others, but as we worship we are brought face-to-face with the realization that unseen eyes know well what we are doing. "All things are naked and open to the eyes of Him to whom we must give account" (Hebrews 4:13).

God's permanent record is not defunct. The apostle John said that unbelievers will have to stand before God's great, white throne. In his vision he saw books opened "and the dead . . . judged according to their works, by the things which were written in the books" (Revelation 21:12). Paul said Christians will have to answer to Christ for the "deeds done in the body" (2 Corinthians 5:10). We are all accountable!

PREPARING TO WORSHIP

Worship is too important to approach casually. It takes thoughtful preparation. True worship pleases God, and when done with a sincere heart, it benefits us as well. If you are the man of the house, you cannot hope to lead your family in this type of worship if you come to your duty unprepared.

Worshiping at church

The man of the house is the worship leader both at home and in the church. Wherever and whenever he leads in worship, he must prepare for it. Much of that preparation will be the same whether for home or the church, but let's think first about preparing to worship at church.

A godly man is challenged to be the role model for his family in public worship. Someone once said, "The best safeguard for the younger generation is a good example by the older generation." Children more often follow what they see than what they are told.

As part of the example he needs to set for his family, the husband and father of the home should demonstrate both commitment and enthusiasm for public worship. This includes attending services and participating in singing, giving, and praying.

Remember the old song that advises, "Don't send your kids to Sunday school, get out of bed and take them"? It appears as if every man of the house hasn't gotten the message yet. One survey found that men constitute only 41 percent of adult church attendees. This is of special concern when linked to a study that Earl Parvin reports in his book *Missions USA*. This study showed that when both parents attend church, 72 percent of their children remain faithful to the church. When the father alone attends, 50 percent of the children remain attendees. But when the mother takes the children to church by herself, only 15 percent remain faithful to the church.[2] The influence you have on your children, Dad, is powerful.

What are some of the things you can do to prepare for public worship? Here are some suggestions.

Make physical preparations

Satan takes great pleasure in destroying the peace and joy you need to enter into worship wholeheartedly. This is true regarding family devotions and the morning church service.

As you may know, Sunday morning can be the worst time of the week. Shoes are lost; clothes need ironing; Sunday school lessons are unfinished; children are tired and cranky. That's why preparing the night before is so important.

Use good sense in scheduling your social engagements or TV viewing on Saturday night. Make sure your family is sufficiently rested for Sunday morning. Treat Saturday night with the same rules you have for a school night, and insist on a reasonable bedtime for the children.

Have everyone lay out the clothes they plan to wear the next day. Place a basket or similar container by the door that leads to your car. Put in it your Bibles, Sunday school lessons, or whatever else you'll need the next morning. This will spare you that last-minute search for things while you hurry out the door.

Many Christians have bought into the "sleep in Sunday" philosophy. They try to catch a few extra winks on Sunday morning and don't get up in time to prepare properly for church. This means their house on Sunday mornings is more like a frantic day at the New York Stock Exchange than a peaceful home.

Let me suggest that you get up at your normal school or work time on Sunday mornings. Have a family breakfast, less hurried than the rest of the week. Include a time of reading the Word and praying with your family. Allow sufficient time for getting ready for church. Don't give your children the impression that going to God's house is an imposition on your weekend.

Build quiet anticipation into preparing for worship. Orthodox Jews get ready for worship on Friday night before they attend their synagogue on Saturday. They light candles, say prayers, and read Scripture. In general, they focus intently on the coming day of worship. Christians could learn some important lessons from their example.

Your physical preparation to worship God reflects your estimation of Him. We communicate that God is of little importance to us if we wait until the last minute and rush around like madmen before meeting Him.

Make spiritual preparations

The role of prayer in preparing for worship can't be overemphasized. You need to pray for yourself, your family, your pastor, and all those who will have a part in the service. If we were to go back to our spiritual roots among our Puritan forefathers, we would find this advice:

> Prepare to meet thy God, O Christian! Betake thyself to thy chamber on the Saturday night . . . The oven of thine heart thus baked, as it were, overnight, would be easily heated the next morning; the fire so well raked up when thou wentest to bed, would be the sooner kindled when thou shouldst rise. If thou wouldst thus leave thy heart with God on the Saturday night, thou shouldst find it with Him in the Lord's Day morning.[3]

Time also should be set aside for soul-searching. The psalmist asks, "Who may ascend into the hill of the LORD? Or who may stand in His holy place?" He answers his own question: "He who has clean hands and a pure heart, who has not lifted up his soul to an idol, nor sworn deceitfully" (Psalm 24:3–4). Sin in our lives short-circuits our ability to connect with God. If there is a faulty connection between God and the worship leader in the house, it will adversely affect the worship potential of the family.

A United Press International release years ago reported a hospital in a Midwestern town that discovered after thirty-five years its fire-fighting equipment had never been connected to the water main. The pipe that led from the building extended four feet underground and stopped! Had firemen needed to use that equipment to put out a blaze, it never would have worked.

Some worshipers are like that incomplete plumbing. They attend church, and on the surface all looks well. But they are disconnected from the One they came to worship. They go through the motions, yet they never experience intimate fellowship with God because sin blocks their way.

We can overcome the inhibitors that Satan uses to block our worship to God. But to do so, we must commit to worship in purity, sincerity, and integrity. Let's think about each of these.

1. *Worship in purity.* In the forests of northern Europe lives a small animal called the ermine. The ermine is brown in the summer, but in the

winter it grows a coat of snow-white fur. Instinctively, the ermine protects his glossy coat from becoming soiled.

Hunters have learned to take advantage of this instinct. Instead of setting a mechanical trap to catch the ermine, they locate the ermine's home in a cleft of a rock or a hollow tree and daub the entrance and the interior with tar. Then their dogs start the chase, and the frightened animal flees toward his home. But finding it covered with dirt, the ermine rejects the only place of safety he has. Rather than dirty his white fur, the ermine courageously faces the yelping dogs, who hold him at bay until the hunters capture him.

The man building a godly home can learn an important lesson from the European ermine. Purity is to be treasured more than life itself.

For the worship leader of the home, keeping the heart pure is an ongoing battle. The apostle Paul speaks of "bringing every thought into captivity to the obedience of Christ" (2 Corinthians 10:5). With God's help, this should be our goal in preparing to worship. You cannot be the worship leader of the home without such cleanliness.

But how do you maintain purity? Our hands get dirty and our hearts do not stay as pure as they ought. What can you do when your life isn't ready for the responsibility of leading your family in worship? Follow the 1 John 1:9 principle: "If we confess our sins, He is faithful and just to forgive us our sins and to cleanse us from all unrighteousness."

"All unrighteousness" is an all-encompassing category; but Jehovah is an all-encompassing God. The secret to recapturing clean hands and a pure heart when they are soiled is confession of sin. The word John chose in Greek for confession is *homologeo*. Literally it means "to say the same thing as another" or "to agree with." When you agree with God that something you have done or said or thought was sin, you have confessed it. And the blood of Jesus Christ cleanses every sin that you confess and turn away from.

When you attribute the highest value possible in your life to God, and you come to worship Him fresh from agreeing that your sin is wrong and are genuinely sorrow for having disobeyed Him, you are ready to worship. That's what purity is all about. Jesus said, "Blessed are the pure in heart, for they shall see God" (Matthew 5:8).

2. *Worship in sincerity.* Have you ever found yourself in this scenario? You are sitting in church with your family beside you on the pew. You

sing with the congregation. You stare at the pastor as he reads the Scriptures. But your mind is focused on a business deal you want to close on Monday. You are not worshiping God; you are worshiping your business.

To worship in sincerity means to worship wholeheartedly, to give your whole heart and mind to the task of showing adoration and respect to the living God. He deserves your undivided attention when you worship Him.

If you find your mind wandering, make it a matter of prayer. Ask God for the power to concentrate on worship. Bring your Bible to church and follow along as the Scriptures are read. Take notes on the sermon. Writing helps focus your attention on the subject at hand.

When you meet with God, in either private or public worship, you must resolve to put your encounter with Him as the most important item on your agenda.

3. *Worship in integrity.* Worship is hindered as well when the guilt of deceitfulness smudges your mind. God wants us to be upright men. The man who wants to deal with Him in an intimate way must first deal with others in integrity.

Richard Helms, in the course of explaining his 1973 testimony during the Watergate hearings, told a Senate panel that despite the fact he had sworn to tell the "whole truth," he believed he had some latitude in the manner in which he gave his answers. As one prosecutor put it, "You can lie without committing perjury; you don't have to tell the whole truth to avoid committing a crime."

God will not accept this type of twisted reasoning. If you do not live before your wife and children in integrity, how can you lead them in the worship of God? It's impossible.

Ted Engstrom tells it straight when he says, "Simply put, integrity is doing what you said you would do. It means you keep your promises. . . . A promise is a holy thing, whether made to the chairman of the board—or to a child." You cannot take your vows lightly and expect God to take you seriously.

Before you load up your wife and kids in the car and start out for church, you should do a reality check on how you have lived up to your promises with them. And while you are at it, how have you lived up to your promises to God?

Integrity is not something we should associate only with business. In fact, some men who would never dream of doing business without integrity never think of leading their homes with that same integrity. Little wonder genuine worship is on the wane in many churches and homes today.

Your unique privilege of being the worship leader in your home is too important to compromise through a lack of preparation. Get yourself ready before you get your family ready.

Worshiping at home

We have looked at the importance of public worship, and those issues are as relevant to men as they are to everyone else. However, the worship leader who wants a godly home faces some special responsibilities there.

The head of the home is responsible to establish a corporate family worship time. This is not the easiest task to accomplish, yet it is one of the most important.

George Gallup Jr. discovered in one of his surveys that "most of those who have ever had religious training in the home remain religious to the end." Religious training in this case does not mean a Christian school education or going to church and Sunday school. The focus is on the home. Church and school are important, but what's done in the home will have the most lasting effect on your family.

To establish your home as a family worship center requires little money but a lot of commitment. There are three basic commitments that the husband and father must make if he is to be the worship leader in the home. They are his commitments to time, place, and content.

Time commitment

The initial hurdle you will face in establishing a family time of worship and devotion to the Lord is finding the hour of the day in which it can take place. Are you having difficulty finding a time that is suitable to everyone in the family? Join the club! Time is not elastic; you cannot stretch it. None of us ever seems to have enough of it. Yet, ironically, we have all there is.

A commitment to finding the time to have family devotions is really a commitment to finding the right time. Every family has 24 hours in each day, 168 hours in every week. Why, then, do some families have a regular time for family worship and others do not? It comes down to commitment. If the worship leader makes a commitment to lead his family in worshiping God at home, he will find the time, in cooperation with the other members of his family.

When my family was young, we struggled with the time issue until, as the worship leader in my home, I sat down with Linda and my children and lovingly but firmly said, "This is something that pleases God. As a family we want to please God more than we want to please friends, coworkers, or anyone else. Let's find a time, even if other things have to go." Once our family made that time commitment, we not only found a time for the Lord each day, but we also found that nothing else had to go.

For you that time may be early in the morning or in the evening. For us, the time was immediately after dinner each night. This became increasingly difficult as our children grew older. There was soccer practice, piano lessons, guys hanging around my daughters—you know all the distractions. But we had made a commitment. We established a time. We worked everything else in life around that time.

For me it meant changing my work habits. For my daughters it meant no phone calls after dinner. For our whole family it meant a new routine: finish dinner, clear the dishes from the table, and go directly to the family room for devotions.

Our family made that commitment more than a decade ago. Now that my family is grown, it still works for Linda and me today because commitments always work. We simply will not permit anything to interfere with our family worship time. Our friends have learned when they call us at that time of day why we don't answer. If it's important, the caller will call back. Not answering the phone is a testimony to our family commitment to regularly worship our God.

Make the commitment. Find a time by working it out with everyone in your family. The worship leader of the family does not make these decisions by fiat. He negotiates them. He makes sure that the time is everyone's best time. That keeps the family motivated to follow the worship leader.

Place commitment

Equally important, although usually not as hard to determine, is the place commitment. Where will you lead your family in worship in the home? What is the best place for all?

Having a place for family devotions doesn't require building an extra room onto your home. You don't have to renovate your house to include a prayer chapel. In fact, you are better off if you don't. Any place will do so long as the family knows that when they meet there, the purpose is to worship the Lord.

The Kroll family found that our family room is the best place. It doesn't have all the religious symbols that our church has, but it has all we need. We could have stayed at the dinner table and read God's Word, but we decided that family devotions should take place in the family room. My children will remember our family room for the times we read God's Word and worshiped Him more than they will for the television programs we watched there.

The place is important because you need to know where things are when you have your family worship time. Just as hunting for your Bible when you are rushing out the door to go to church kills the spirit of worship, so, too, does hunting for your Bible when you want to have family devotions.

Content commitment

The time and place are important, but they are secondary. The most important matter is what takes place during that time and in that place. The man who wants to build a godly home needs to make sure that worship actually occurs. Depending on the age of the children involved, the content may vary, but the content should be structured. As my children grew older, our family altar content grew with them.

A number of books are available to assist you in planning a family worship time. The worship leader, however, must start the process and keep it going. This doesn't mean that you dominate the devotional time. Assigning different tasks to involve others is a good way to keep their interest. But God does hold you responsible for seeing that it takes place.

Your family may be very different from mine. I tell you the way we did it only as an example. It's not better than another way; it was just our way.

We had three basic tools for our family devotions, and we kept them in our family room permanently. First, each of us had a Bible. We read a chapter or two per night. We commented on what the passage meant to us, what we learned most from it, and how we could apply it in our lives. Sometimes we simply asked each other questions about the passage. As worship leader in my home, I wanted my family to do more than read the Word; I wanted them to meditate upon it and apply it to their lives.

Second, we kept a copy of Patrick Johnstone's *Operation World* with our Bibles. Each night we read about a different country, learned all we could about its spiritual needs, and then prayed for the requests that various mission agencies working in that country had. We also kept an atlas in our family room. If anyone was unsure where in the world a country was, we enjoyed a little geography lesson. It was surprising how much about the world we all learned just through our family worship time.

Third, we kept a variety of prayer reminders in a basket. We chose several to pray for each night along with the requests for the country we studied that evening. These prayer reminders included Back to the Bible's *Strategic Prayer Focus* and similar prayer bulletins from other ministries. We also included prayer cards from missionary friends.

Each year at Christmas my family received (and still receives) many greeting cards. We used to enjoy them through the holiday season and then discard them. But I found a better use for them. Now during the holidays, we keep them in our prayer basket, choose one each night, and pray for those who sent greetings to us. It's a great way to make our prayer time personal and to remember our friends and family in prayer throughout the year.

Finally, we always made sure that our family devotions included huge helpings of praise and worship. This is not a time to get to know God's Word, but to get to know God. It is not a time to be thankful for friends, but to be thankful to God for friends. It is a time of worship, a time to tell God how worthwhile and valuable He is to us as a family.

GETTING IT TOGETHER

Worship is the greatest privilege any human can experience. If you are going to be a real man, you must lead your family in this arena of life as well. Certainly it takes effort, sometimes almost superhuman effort. Most things that are worthwhile do. But what an opportunity!

In Kandy, Sri Lanka, one of the most spectacular festivals of the Buddhist world takes place during August. On the appointed night a procession of forty elephants, richly bedecked with silver, gold, and jeweled embroidery and smothered with flowers, solemnly tread a mile-long, lighted route. The air is filled with the noise of yelling and shrieking crowds, wailing pipes, clanging symbols, and the honking of countless conch shells. The object of all this attention is a bejeweled casket, carried by the lead elephant, supposedly containing a two-inch-long discolored eyetooth reclaimed from Buddha's funeral pyre in 543 B.C. and brought to Sri Lanka eight hundred years later.

Incredible, isn't it? To think that so many people would go to so much trouble and sacrifice just to pay homage to a tooth of a man who died and was cremated more than twenty-five hundred years ago.

What a challenge to those whom God has appointed as the worship leaders in their homes. If others can make such ado over a tooth, how much more should we feel compelled to lead our family in the worship of the true and living God. After all, only He is worthy.

[1] J. Oswald Sanders, *Spiritual Problems* (Chicago: Moody Press, 1971), p. 138.

[2] Earl Parvin, *Missons USA* (Chicago: Moody Press, 1985), p. 232.

[3] J. I. Packer, *A Quest for Godliness* (Wheaton, Ill.: Crossway Books, 1990), p. 257.

Chapter 6

THE PRIEST IN HIS HOME

A class of first-graders was drawing pictures of what they thought God looked like. Some of the young artists were highly imaginative. Their pictures featured everything from rainbows to Superman. But one little girl's drawing was unique. When asked about it she said, "I don't know what God looks like, so I drew a picture of my daddy."

In many ways this little girl was right. A child is not likely to find a father in God unless he first finds something of God in his father.

Being a real man in the home means more than being the bread winner. God has given you the responsibility of being His representative to the family. Perhaps of even greater importance, He has given you the responsibility of representing your family to God. In biblical terms we call such a person a priest.

THE PRIESTS OF GOD

The Old Testament priests were the official ministers or worship leaders of Israel. This responsibility meant they had many duties to perform. Priests officiated at temple worship by leading the people to confess their sins. As the teachers of the Law to the people, they were the messengers of the Lord (Malachi 2:7). But far and away their most important priestly role was as mediators between man and God. The priests offered sacrifices so the sins of the people might be forgiven (Leviticus 4:20, 26, 31). They stood between God and men, praying for men to be acceptable to God.

The high priest was more than just the head priest. He was the ruler of the house of God, the supreme religious leader of his people. He held a position above all others. The high priest was distinguished from his fellow priests by the clothes he wore, the duties he performed, and the particular requirements placed upon him as the spiritual head of God's people.

The New Testament, especially Hebrews, portrays Jesus as the ultimate High Priest. "Therefore, in all things He had to be made like His brethren, that He might be a merciful and faithful High Priest in things pertaining to God, to make propitiation for the sins of the people. . . .

Therefore, holy brethren, partakers of the heavenly calling, consider the Apostle and High Priest of our confession, Christ Jesus" (Hebrews 2:17; 3:1).

Jesus did more than offer a sacrifice that was acceptable to God; He was the sacrifice. He offered Himself as an atonement to God for our sin, once and for all. Having paid for our sins, Jesus now fulfills the ministry of intercession for us. Hebrews 7:25 says, "Therefore He is also able to save to the uttermost those who come to God through Him, since He always lives to make intercession for them."

Jesus is our High Priest. He alone could offer a sacrifice that would be acceptable to God—His own precious blood. You cannot offer anything that will save your family from their sins. But that's not what you are called to do. Fathers are to be priests in their homes, not high priests. You can be an effective channel to God for your family by using the access provided by the one and only High Priest—Jesus Christ. This special relationship is reserved for the head of the home.

DAD THE PRIEST

When men think of building a godly home, they often forget their role as priest. Most people think of priests as men who sit in booths and hear confessions. Yet that is not what the Bible says about the priest.

From the earliest ages, fathers functioned as priests for the family, even before the development of the priesthood. The first thing Noah did when he left the ark was to build an altar and sacrifice to God (Genesis 8:20). Job sacrificed on behalf of his children (Job 1:5). The night of the Passover in Egypt, each man was to sacrifice a lamb for his family—one lamb, one family. This met God's requirement for a blood atonement (Exodus 12:3).

Later, when the priesthood was established in Israel and laymen no longer served at the altar, the father's spiritual role was redefined. Still, he continued to be the priestly leader in his home.

Dads no longer offer sacrifices because Jesus took care of that. Hebrews 10:12 says that Jesus, "after He had offered one sacrifice for sins forever, sat down at the right hand of God." The one priestly function that you still need to perform, however, is that of prayer. If Jesus continually intercedes for His people, it must be important for you to intercede continually for your family as well.

Prayer is the wonderful privilege of every Christian, but it is a necessity for the family priest. As others have said, you can do more than pray, but you can't do more until you have prayed. If you want to see your family move forward for God, if you want to see existing situations change and lives turn around, then you must assume your role as priest in the home. The fervent prayers of godly men move the hand of God.

What shall the priest in the home pray for? Who should be the object of a father's continual supplications? God's Word helps us discern these responsibilities.

Pray for yourself

Do you think it is selfish for the family priest to pray for himself? Is it selfish for him to pray that he will be a man of God? Is it selfish to pray that he will be the godly leader of his home? Not in the least. In fact, failure to rely on God is the height of selfishness. Praying for yourself is one way to admit that you can't make it on your own.

Your role as the man of the house is too important not to have God's help. Don't hesitate to ask for it. Ask Him to reveal through His Word what it takes to succeed as a father. Ask Him how to stay near to His heart. Ask God to give you a thirsting for godliness that can be quenched only by His Spirit.

Pray that God will equip you to be that complete husband and father for which He designed you. Pray for wisdom in your relationship with your wife. Pray for direction in raising your children. Pray for the power of His Holy Spirit in your role as man of the house. We need all the help we can get, and the greatest help possible is just a prayer away.

You don't pray for yourself to increase your importance; you are already important to God and to your family. Instead, you pray for yourself to be a priest fit to pray for your family.

Dream big and pray big. Gold was discovered in the Sacramento Valley in January 1848. Within three months, the hills swarmed with more than four thousand men seeking their fortunes. By the end of the year, some fifty thousand gold seekers were staking their claims. Each one had to face tremendous odds—inclement weather, hostile Indians, disease. But they came because they dreamed of striking it rich. Not many of them achieved that dream, but they did accomplish something even greater: they facilitated the founding of California.

Don't be afraid to make your prayers as big as your dreams. Too often we treat God like a pauper unable to grant anything but the most miniscule requests. We relegate prayer to the small, tangible things of life—food on the table, house payments, health, safety, etc. But there are much larger issues to be concerned with as well. The well-known nineteenth-century pastor Phillips Brooks admonished, "Do not pray for easy lives; pray to be stronger men. Do not pray for tasks equal to your powers; pray for power equal to your tasks."

Being the priestly father is an awesome task. The challenges facing the family in society are tremendous. Only God is bigger than these challenges. But you can take up the same confident phrase that the apostle Paul used, "I can do all things through Christ who strengthens me" (Philippians 4:13).

A colony of ants once lived by a railroad track. Several times a day trains hurtled down those rails and shook the ant hill to its foundations. One day the queen ant decided she could not put up with it anymore. "I'm going up and giving the engineer a piece of my mind," she declared. Taking her stand upon the rails, she waited. Finally a train came rumbling down the track, and she was never heard from again.

There are some fast trains bearing down upon us that seem overwhelming. Drugs, sex, and alcohol are destroying family after family. The trials in raising a godly family in today's society seem to overtake us faster than a speeding locomotive. They make us feel like a tiny ant on the tracks, waiting certain destruction. Yet if you pray for yourself and seek the help of God in raising your family, you will soon learn that you aren't the ant; you are the locomotive. No ant is a match for the Engineer of your train. Scripture says, "You are of God, little children, and have overcome them, because He who is in you is greater than he who is in the world" (1 John 4:4).

When David faced Goliath, he must have looked like an ant in the shadow of that great giant. But he prayed for God's help and felled Goliath like a train squashes an ant (1 Samuel 17:45–51). When Daniel was on the spot with Nebuchadnezzar, the first thing he did was pray (Daniel 2:17–18). When Elijah faced the impossible task of raising a young boy from the dead, the first thing he did was—you guessed it—pray (1 Kings 17:21).

Learn to commit yourself and your inabilities and inadequacies to God, and let Him make a winner out of you. Cast yourself upon God. Confess to Him your weaknesses. Agree with Him that apart from the empowering of His Holy Spirit you can do nothing (John 15:5). Acknowledge your utter dependency upon His power, and then watch out: the ants in your life will be in a precarious position indeed.

Pray for your family

The family as an institution is in trouble, and fathers must take much of the blame. Many men today have become absentee dads. They are never around, never available to their family, never the priest of their home.

A cartoon showed a little boy looking up at his mother, who was holding a young child and pregnant with yet a third. The boy was asking, "Mommy, where do daddies come from?" Somehow the humor gets lost in the tragedy.

The absentee father is tearing American families apart. A vacuum exists where there should be a priest. The family needs a rock, but many are finding only shifting sand. So prevalent is the phenomenon of absentee fathers that many women have concluded that dear old dad is unnecessary and they purposely bear children out of wedlock.

Some time ago one of the television networks aired a three-day series of reports on teen pregnancy. The second day focused on a family consisting of a grandmother, a mother, and a ninth-grade daughter who had a baby of her own. When asked if a father was necessary in raising a family, the mother emphatically said, "No. I raised my daughter without one." Looking at the result, one might question the mother's insight.

Some fathers are very different. They provide adequately for their family; they see that their children receive a good education; they even come home every night. But they come home only at night—late at night. One mother told of hearing her preschool son talking to another four-year-old boy on the front steps. "Where is your daddy?" he asked. "I've never seen him." "Oh, he doesn't live here," came the reply. "He only sleeps here." Many absentee dads are married to their job and give their greatest attention and energy to their clients, their boss, or their projects. And the family suffers.

While these dads claim that success at home is more important to them than success at work, 64 percent of them admit they are workaholics—addicted to success on the job. In one survey men indicated that having a happy family life ranked as more important than having enough money (25 percent versus 21 percent). Yet these same men said their jobs had a negative effect on their family. An absentee dad is not much better than no dad at all.

Whether gone because of work commitments, divorce, or neglect, absentee fathers are creating a ripple effect felt throughout our society. The National Father Center reported, "One of the consequences of the sense of fatherlessness was identified recently by a vice chief of police of Los Angeles. He claimed that a chief characteristic of boys who joined street gangs was the absence of a father; the gangs provided a sense of protection and commitment which the absent father did not."[1]

There is much for the man who would be priest to his family to pray about. Pray for God's protection for your family. Pray for family unity, especially during the challenging years when you are raising teenagers. My wife and I always have made our family a priority second only to God. I believe my children have sensed that. They are grown and gone now, but I pray there will never be a time when they won't look forward to coming home to Linda and me.

If your family is falling apart, don't take the restorative power of prayer lightly. It's a much greater weapon than you realize. If your family is holding together, don't take the preventative power of prayer frivolously either. Your family is too important for the family priest to quit praying for them.

Pray for your wife

When was the last time you prayed with your wife? That could be an embarrassing question. Here's a potentially more embarrassing one. When was the last time you prayed for your wife?

Many men not only fail to pray with their wives, but they also fail to pray for them. What a truly wonderful experience they are missing, an experience that could bring them closer to their wife than any marriage seminar or counseling session could.

Prayer creates intimacy. Many men and women are settling today for physical relationships when what they really want is true intimacy. When Josh McDowell spoke at Moody Founder's Week some years ago, he said,

A little over a year ago I debated the cofounder of *Playboy* on television for three hours. He agreed with me on this point. My statement was this: "We have not been through a sexual revolution. . . . What we have been through in the last fifteen years has been a revolution in the search for intimacy. Most of our young people do not want the physical aspect of sex; they want someone who cares. They want to be able to care. They want intimacy. We have allowed our culture to dictate to us that the only way you find intimacy is through the physical—and that's an absolute lie!"[2]

Adults—including married couples—are looking for the same thing. If we could see beneath the facade, we would find many wives shriveling up on the inside because they lack this deeper intimacy in their marriage relationship. Furthermore, if husbands love their wives and are aware of their longing, they are likely scratching their head trying to figure out a way to achieve this intimacy.

As is usually the case, sex is not the answer. Even secular psychologists agree that Sigmund Freud didn't have the answers to men's and women's deepest needs. Sex is important in marriage, but it is not the key to intimacy and happiness that Hollywood would have us believe.

But God has the answer to increased non-physical intimacy in a marriage. It is prayer—praying for the one you love, with the one you love.

When we pray for and/or with someone, a bonding occurs that goes far beyond the physical. Our souls become knit together in an intimate relationship that cannot be accomplished any other way. Edwin Cole, author of *Maximized Manhood*, comments, "Men who know their wives in prayer also know them in the living room, kitchen, and bedroom."[3]

The priest in the home has only one family and only one spouse to pray for. That means you can concentrate your prayers and, consequently, concentrate your intimacy. Pray for your wife; pray with your wife. Let her hear your love and concern for her as you express it to God. It's a win-win-win situation: you win, she wins, you win together.

Prayer heals bitterness. It's a proven fact that you can't pray sincerely for someone and remain bitter toward him. The Bible says, "Be angry, and do not sin: do not let the sun go down on your wrath" (Ephesians 4:26).

I had a friend whose marriage was characterized by a harmony not often seen between married couples. When asked what the secret to his relationship was, he replied, "My wife and I always have a prayer time together before we go to bed. That way everything gets taken care of before we go to sleep."

If you work out disagreements before you go to bed, you will never end up sleeping with the enemy. If you work out those disagreements before you go to bed, you will never find reason not to pray for your spouse before you fall asleep each night.

God does not allow us to pray vindictively. I read of an elderly couple who had been miserable together for years. Finally the wife confronted her husband. "Frank, we've been miserable together for forty years. The only solution I see is for the Lord to take one of us home. I just want you to know that when He answers that prayer, I plan to go live with my sister in Buffalo."

I'm sure this was written tongue in cheek; God doesn't answer those kinds of prayers. What He will do, however, is heal hurting relationships. Yet you must want that healing, you must be willing to work to bring it about, and you must be willing to pray for God's help.

As you pray for your spouse, you become concerned about what's best for her. As you concentrate on the good that you want to see done in her life, those traits that currently irritate you tend to fade into the background and eventually become unimportant.

Is your spouse the closest person to you? Does she mean more to you than anything else in the world? If you said yes (and I hope you did), why would you not pray for a treasure so dear to you? Why would any of us neglect to pray for the one who touches our soul more deeply than any other? It's a shame we are sometimes so busy with our jobs and so detached from our families that we forget to pray for the ones who mean the most to us.

Don't let it happen to you. Today, establish a time when your spouse and you pray with each other. Hold hands if you like. But don't just pray with her; pray for her too! She'll love you for it.

Prayer promotes unity. Unity comes to your marriage when focus comes to your prayers. As you pray for those things that concern your wife, her concerns become your concerns. This doesn't mean you become uniform or that you always agree. If two people always agree, one of them is not necessary. No, differences are what make marriages interesting. But prayer works like a harness on a team of horses. Each horse is different, but the harness enables them to pull together. Through prayer the husband-wife differences become a source of unity and strength.

A number of years ago I saw a cartoon showing a woman in a lawyer's office. The caption read, "I married my ideal but he's become an ordeal and now I want a new deal." Does that sound like you? It happens all too frequently.

The differences that drew people together often become the problems that split them apart. When they were dating, she was enamored by his strong, silent personality. After they were married, she became frustrated because he never communicated. During the courtship, he was thrilled with her fun-loving personality. After marriage he complained that she never grew up.

There is some truth that opposites attract. We see characteristics in others that we lack, and that is what draws us to them. God's desire is for these differences to enrich our lives. He wants the husband and wife to complement each other. Instead, we allow our differences to become walls between us.

What's the solution? Certainly one answer is for the husband and father of the home to be the priest of his family and spend time each day in the ministry of priestly prayer. As you bring the one God gave you before His throne of grace, the Lord will bind your hearts together with His. Scripture says, "Though one may be overpowered by another, two can withstand him. And a threefold cord is not quickly broken" (Ecclesiastes 4:12). There is hardly a better analogy for a godly marriage. When you keep God involved in the marriage equation, He creates a relationship that can stand the stress and strain of time.

Pray for your children

Most fathers feel a strong responsibility to provide for their children. They work long hours and make sacrifices so their sons and daughters can have material possessions. But we need to heed what Martin Luther said centuries ago: "We certainly want to provide not only for our children's bellies but for their souls."

To paraphrase Jesus' words in Mark 8:36: "What good is it if we give our children everything they want in this world and let them lose their souls?" Does it make any eternal sense to provide those things for your family that last only days or years but fail to provide those things that last forever? Yet many men are doing that, even as they read these words. As the priest of your home, you should be more concerned with the spiritual welfare of your children than getting them into the college of their choice.

What will you pray for when you bring your children before God? Here are a few suggestions.

Pray for their salvation. Do you want to see your children trust Christ as Savior? Of course you do. You can give them many opportunities to hear the Gospel. You can enroll them in Sunday school, take them to AWANA or youth group, and encourage them to read and memorize Bible verses. But all of this is like trying to drive a car without gasoline unless you also pray for them. Only God's Spirit can draw your child to the Savior, but prayer prepares the way for the Spirit's work of grace.

Many famous Christians came to know Christ at a young age. Polycarp, one of the apostolic fathers and an early Christian martyr, became a believer at the age of nine. Sir Isaac Watts, the noted hymn writer, professed his faith when he, too, was nine. Matthew Henry, known as the Prince of Commentators, received Christ when he was eleven. Jonathan Edwards, a famous preacher and theologian, made his commitment at the young age of seven. You can be sure that these men had priestly fathers who prayed for them.

I remember the night I chose to receive Christ as if it happened only yesterday. I was five when a children's evangelist came to our town. He was conducting a children's crusade in the church pastored by my father. One night when he gave the invitation, I realized my need to have my sins forgiven, and I came forward to trust Jesus Christ as my Savior. I understood everything I needed to. But one thing I didn't understand at the time was how much my parents had been praying for this day since I was born.

Pray for the salvation of your children and grandchildren—even your great-grandchildren. James Dobson claims that four generations in his family have come to know Christ because of the prayers of his grandfather. You have no more important responsibility in life than to pray for the next generations.

Pray for their spiritual growth. Earlier I alluded to the Old Testament man named Job. He was a family man, with seven sons and three daughters. They were a close-knit family. Job 1:4 says, "Now his sons would go and feast in their houses, each on his appointed day, and would send and invite their three sisters to eat and drink with them."

Job loved his family. He loved them too much not to assume the role of priest in the home. He took that responsibility much more seriously than most fathers do today. Verse 5 says, "So it was, when the days of feasting had run their course, that Job would send and sanctify them, and he would rise early in the morning and offer burnt offerings according to the number of them all. For Job said, 'It may be that my sons have sinned and cursed God in their hearts.' Thus Job did regularly."

Was Job a busy man? Without a doubt. He was a business tycoon with vast holdings. Today we would say he was involved in agribusiness. He had sheep and camels and servants and all sorts of demands upon his time. But with all his responsibilities, he never missed praying for his children.

You cannot forgive your children's sins; only God can do that. But you can pray that God will move in His sovereign way to bring them to repentance. That's what Job did; it's something any priest of the family can do.

We aren't told what the father of the prodigal son did while he waited for his boy to come home again (Luke 15:11–32), but what do you suppose the chances are he failed to pray? Not likely. I suspect there was never an hour that didn't find a prayer on his lips for his wayward son. Little wonder there was rejoicing when the boy came home. His return was an answer to prayer!

Pray for your child, especially if you know he is living in a way that displeases God. As the priest of your home, pray that he will not have it easy away from God. Pray that he will be convicted of his sins and understand what he must do. Pray that he will repent. If he has already left home, pray that he will come home again.

And don't forget, when you pray you hope. The two go hand in hand. So pray hard, hope hard, and keep an eye on the door. You soon may see someone there you love.

If you are not praying for your children, you are not helping their spiritual growth. If you are not helping them grow spiritually, then you are hindering their growth. There is no neutral ground.

Pray for their service. As a parent, it's wonderful to know all your children are saved. But your priestly prayer responsibilities do not stop there. If salvation were all there is, God in His mercy would take them home to heaven as soon as they were saved. Instead, God has a plan for their lives. He saved them so they will serve Him.

It is the duty of the priest of the house to pray for God to reveal His plan of service to his sons and daughters. Jesus said, "The harvest truly is plentiful, but the laborers are few. Therefore pray the Lord of the harvest to send out laborers into His harvest" (Matthew 9:38).

We're good at praying that request for someone else's children, but what about our own? Do you hide your children when a missionary speaker comes to church with a challenge to missions? Do you counsel them to pursue a career that will allow them to make a good living? I can't think of any more eternally damaging advice.

One of my responsibilities as the priest of my home is to pray that God will use each of my children mightily in His service. I always have prayed that God would call each of them into lifetime ministry for Him. Now, He may not do that. That may not be His will. But I can trust God with my children. I give them to Him for His service. If He doesn't want to use them in this way, He'll give them back. I can trust Him to do what's best for my loved ones.

Could one of those laborers you pray about be your son or daughter? It is difficult to watch your child leave home, knowing that you will not see him as frequently as you would like. But distance is nowhere near the problem that disobedience is. It would be far worse to see him out of God's will.

John Barkman says we should pray for our children "before they understand, until they understand, and then because they understand."[4] That's the job of the family priest.

Pray for your grandchildren

You've heard parents say, "If I had known grandchildren were so much fun I would have had them first." As a grandfather of six beautiful granddaughters and four handsome grandsons, I'm beginning to appreciate the feeling. More important, I have an added responsibility as the priest in my home. Now I have ten more precious gifts from God to pray for.

Next to their parents, grandparents are the most important people in a child's life. Sometimes grandparents have more time to spend with their grandchildren than their parents do. They also have more time to pray.

Eight of my grandchildren are distant from me here in Nebraska—they live in North Carolina and Virginia. So my prayers are all long-distance prayers for them. Two of my grandchildren live nearby. But they are all my family, just as much as their parents are. If I am to take my responsibilities as priest in the home seriously, I must be the priest for every member of my extended family, not just the next generation.

And this responsibility did not begin with me. My father and mother pray daily for Linda and me, for their grandchildren, and for their great-grandchildren. They, too, do not have the opportunity to spend time with their grandchildren or great-grandchildren, but they now have some extra golden hours to pray for them.

In European and Asian societies, three or more generations of a family live under the same roof. Here in America that is rarely the case. Have we lost touch with the generations of our family by being such a mobile society? Maybe so, but that should not hinder our priesthood. Men who are the priests of their family are the priests of as many generations as are living. It's a big responsibility, Grandpa, but also a great joy.

AN ONGOING RESPONSIBILITY

The Old Testament priests were appointed for life. Only when they became too disabled to perform their function or they died were they released from their responsibilities. Should our families expect anything less from us?

The older I grow, the more important prayer becomes to me. And the longer I am a priest in the home, the more important praying for my family becomes. My children never stop appreciating a dad who prays for them. Neither will yours, even if they don't say so.

I remember years ago when I took a little break from writing so I could watch a football game on television. I turned the computer off and left it for several hours. When I returned there was a little card on the keyboard from Tiffany, my youngest daughter. She had visited my study and left a card that read: "Anyone can be a father, but it takes someone special to be a dad."

She knows that a day never goes by that I do not pray for her and the rest of my family. It is my joy; it is my privilege; it is my ongoing responsibility. After all, I am a priest to my family.

The priestly temple has been destroyed. The priestly sacrifices are irrelevant. But Dad, your priestly prayers are still necessary. Your family is counting on you. Be a real man; be your family's priest.

[1] *Homemade*, Vol. 16, #5, May 1992.

[2] Josh McDowell, Moody Founder's Week, Chicago, Ill., 1986.

[3] Edwin Louis Cole, *Maximized Manhood* (Springdale, Pa.: Whitaker House, 1982), p. 79.

[4] John Barkman, *Briercrest Echo*, June 1983.

Chapter 7

THE PROVIDER IN HIS HOME

The comic strip "Herman" featured him lying on a psychiatrist's couch in deep despair. His psychiatrist says, "I'm having a difficult time understanding the source of your anxiety. You have a luxury townhouse, a motor home, three cars, a powerboat, all the latest stereo and video equipment, and you're planning another vacation in Hawaii. What's the problem?"

With a sigh Herman replies, "I only make $85 a week."

I wonder if Herman is also in charge of our government's spending. As of March 2001, our government was in debt for more than $5.7 trillion. If that were divided between each person in the United States, every individual would owe over $20,000. Furthermore, the national debt has continued to increase an average of $123 million per day since September 1999.[1]

Back when the debt was "only" about $4 trillion, *USA Today* illustrated the situation this way. On September 18, 1789, Alexander Hamilton, then U.S. Secretary of the Treasury, took out the first government loan for $191,608.81. He promptly repaid it in nine months. Let's assume that you earned the same amount of money every hour that Hamilton borrowed some two hundred years ago and put it all toward that debt. How long do you think it would take you to repay $4 trillion? Five hundred years? One thousand years? Try 2,610 years! You can imagine how much longer the extra trillion and a half has made that pay-off time.

No wonder someone said, "A penny saved is a congressional oversight." The United States government is caught in an economic quagmire, but it couldn't have happened without at least the tacit consent of taxpayers. Money management on the government level has to start with sound financial decisions made by individual families.

A spendthrift attitude is not only reflected in our government but in our homes. According to one source, in 1998 the national consumer debt reached an all-time high of more than $1 trillion. It's no wonder that the fiscal year ending June 30, 1996, saw more than one million personal bankruptcies for the first time ever in a twelve-month period. Two years later almost one and a half million personal bankruptcies were filed. Nearly half the households in the United States claim they are having difficulty making even the minimum monthly payments on their credit cards.[2] Larry Burkett, a Christian financial advisor, says nine out of ten people who earn a paycheck do not know how to spend it wisely.

God has given you, as the leader in the home, the responsibility of being the provider. In fact, the apostle Paul states that a man who does not provide for his family "has denied the faith and is worse than an unbeliever" (1 Timothy 5:8). I don't mean to imply that providing for one's family only involves money. It takes more than dollars and cents to meet the needs of your loved ones.

Christina Onassis, who died in 1988 at the age of thirty-seven, once said, "Happiness is not based on money, and the greatest proof of that is our family!" A friend observed after Ms. Onassis's tragic death, "She had houses all over the world, but she never really had a home."[3]

In 1972 West German industrialist Friedrich Flick died. He left an estate valued at approximately $1.5 billion. Flick was totally dedicated to his business empire. Employees say that he buried his wife at 3 P.M. one day in 1966 and was back to work two hours later. When Herr Flick died, his family disintegrated into bickering and quarreling factions. He had amassed a fortune but failed to create a family who could get along with each other. As one observer put it, "Flick hit home runs at the office, but he struck out at home!"[4]

YOUR ATTITUDE TOWARD MONEY

God wants you to provide a home. This takes love, commitment, and personal leadership.

Having said that, we still need to realize it also takes money. God is concerned about your finances—as indicated by the more than seven hundred references to money in the Scriptures. Nearly two-thirds of Jesus' parables deal with wealth in one form or another. What God takes seriously, we should take seriously too. His attitude toward the stewardship of our possessions can be summed up in three principles. Let's think about them.

Be concerned but not preoccupied

It would be foolish not to be concerned about our material needs. The Book of Proverbs says, "Go to the ant, you sluggard! Consider her ways and be wise, which, having no captain, overseer or ruler, provides her supplies in the summer and gathers her food in the harvest. How long will you slumber, O sluggard? When will you rise from your sleep? A little sleep, a little slumber, a little folding of the hands to sleep—so shall your poverty come on you like a robber, and your need like an armed man" (6:6–11).

It's expensive to live these days. Some say the situation is so bad that money no longer speaks; it's gone before it has a chance to say anything. In an article for *USA Today*, Tim Friend noted that 87 percent of parents report that they have financial difficulties.

For a child born in 1990 and raised to the age of seventeen, the U.S. Department of Agriculture projected that the average cost would be $210,070. It now estimates that a child born in 1999 will cost about $160,140 ($237,000 when adjusted for inflation) to raise to the age of seventeen (that includes $53,310 for housing and $27,990 for food).[5] Any way you look at it, that's a lot of money!

Yet to allow your concern to become preoccupation would be wrong. Jesus said, "No one can serve two masters; for either he will hate the one and love the other, or else he will be loyal to the one and despise the other. You cannot serve God and mammon. Therefore I say to you, do not worry about your life, what you will eat or what you will drink; nor about your body, what you will put on. Is not life more than food and the body more than clothing?" (Matthew 6:24–25).

When you become preoccupied with money (either because you have too much or you have too little), it takes first place in your life. It dominates your thinking, and that's idolatry. Only God can legitimately fill your thoughts. When something pushes Him into the background, you have broken the first commandment: "You shall have no other gods before Me" (Exodus 20:3).

Money is a good servant but a poor master. Those whose lives have been ruled by money are not enviable. J. Paul Getty was one of the wealthiest men of his time. His personal possessions totaled more than $4 billion. Yet the *Los Angeles Times* quoted Mr. Getty as saying in his autobiography, "I have never been given to envy . . . save for the envy I feel toward those people who have the ability to make a marriage work and endure happily. It's an art I have never been able to master. My record: five marriages, five divorces. In short, five failures."

Mr. Getty also had a son addicted to heroine, a grandson mutilated by kidnappers who demanded a ransom of $2.9 million, and a granddaughter with AIDS. Billions of dollars did nothing to bring contentment and joy to this family.

Some people have allowed a preoccupation with money to ruin their lives in other ways. Hetty Green is one of the most famous misers in American history. When she died in 1916, she left a $100 million estate. But she ate cold oatmeal in order to save the expense of heating water. The doctors amputated her son's leg because she took so long to find a free clinic that advanced infection made it impossible to save. Even her own death is attributed to a fit of apoplexy brought on by arguing over the value of buying skim milk versus whole milk because it was cheaper.

These people and thousands like them allowed their preoccupation with money to ruin their opportunity to live a full life. It's often said that we are to love people and use things. When money becomes your idol, you end up using people and loving things.

If reality doesn't strike before, it does when you face the ultimate experience of mankind—death. Possessions show their true value when you are faced with the likelihood of your demise.

A wealthy woman was in one of the lifeboats ready to cast off from the *Titanic* when she asked for a moment to get something from her room. She quickly returned carrying not her money or jewels but three oranges. Hours earlier she would have thought nothing about the fruit, but now they had become precious to her.

A wealthy man lay in his palatial home dying. His family gathered around and asked if there were any last requests. "Yes," the man said, "I would like to take one last ride." "Do you want to ride in your Cadillac or your Corvette?" his solicitous wife asked. "Neither," he replied. "I want a very small camel and a very large needle."

Jesus told His disciples, "And again I say to you, it is easier for a camel to go through the eye of a needle than for a rich man to enter the kingdom of God" (Matthew 19:24). God wants to do more than give you money; He wants to make you wealthy. When our hearts and hands are full of earthly treasures, He can't give us those things that have eternal value.

Be wise but not stingy

Scripture commands us to "be wise as serpents" (Matthew 10:16). The provider in the home is responsible to devise a way to use those provisions wisely. This requires some form of a budget. Some may protest and say, "I don't have enough money to budget!" Actually, the less you have, the more you need to budget. Those who are barely getting by (or not at all) on their present income need to know where every penny goes. The best way to do that is to devise a budget. It's not my purpose to go into the details of budgeting, but there are some general rules that should be remembered.

Before constructing a budget, keep track of your expenses for a month or two. This will give you some idea of your current spending habits. If a budget is going to work, it has to fit your needs and not the other way around. Find out how you are really spending your money, and then with the input of your spouse (or better yet, the whole family), consider how you might make changes to get your expenses in line with your income. Ben Franklin once said there are only two ways of solving money problems: earn more or spend less. Perhaps in your situation you will have to do both.

Once you've constructed your budget, each one in the family needs to make a commitment to do his part in keeping his expenses within the guidelines. A budget won't work unless you work your budget. While a budget shouldn't be viewed as a straight jacket, deviations should be justifiable and a plan made to compensate for the difference.

Furthermore, give your budget time to work. Everything—new shoes, new cars, new computers—requires breaking in. You have to work out the squeaks, the clunks, and the bugs before they feel natural. The same is true for a budget. One goal of a budget is to set aside a little each month for those annual and semiannual expenses such as car insurance or taxes. This means during the first year of your budget you will hit those obligations before you've had the time to totally save for them. That's OK. It doesn't mean your budget isn't working (you'll have something put away to help). By the time those expenses roll around the next year, you'll have the whole amount in a savings account drawing interest.

Numerous books deal with the issue of budgeting for Christians. A couple that I recommend are Larry Burkett's *Debt-Free Living* and Ron Blue's *Master Your Money*. Check with your local Christian bookstore to see what other books are available. You may also want to visit Crown Financial Ministries on the Web at www.crown.org.

Savings also need to play an important role in your financial planning. But be careful: not all savings plans are created equal. You could become like the housewife who was approached by a refrigerator salesman. The man assured her, "Lady, you can save enough on your food bill to pay for it." The housewife replied, "Well, sir, we're paying for a car on the carfare we save, we're paying for a washing machine on the laundry bill we save, and we're paying for a television set on the cost of movies we don't see anymore. It looks as if we can't afford to save any more money at this time."

Often we feel we can't afford to save, but in reality we can't afford not to save. Sir John Templeton, founder of the multibillion-dollar Templeton Mutual Funds company, was asked, "To what do you attribute your tremendous success?" He replied, "The Lord and disciplined saving." He went on to describe how he and his wife had saved 50 percent of their meager earnings early in their married life. They once furnished an apartment for $25 by buying at auctions and secondhand stores. They drove used cars, lived in rented apartments, and rarely ate out until his income was well established.

It's never too late to start saving, but equally true, it's never too early. Not only does it result in a financial benefit, but developing discipline in one area makes it easier to be disciplined in other areas of our lives.

When you set up your savings plan, you need to include short-term goals such as vacations, birthdays, and Christmas. This puts automatic spending limits on these occasions. You can't buy Aunt Myrtle that $150 angora sweater if you've saved only $50. Also, saving prevents the common after-vacation or after-Christmas blues that come in the mail with your bills from MasterCard or Visa.

In addition, you need to have long-term savings goals. This might include saving for a replacement car or an extra vehicle. Some financial managers suggest that when you pay off a car, continue to make the payment but put it into a savings account. Hopefully, your automobile will hang together until that account has grown large enough to pay cash for the next one.

Don't forget that appliances wear out eventually too. Check with an appliance dealer to see what the average life span of your machine should be, and then calculate the replacement cost, adding something for inflation. By putting away that small amount each month, the money will be available when it is needed.

Every budget should have a category for giving. The apostle Paul said, "On the first day of the week let each one of you lay something aside, storing up as he may prosper, that there be no collections when I come" (1 Corinthians 16:2). The first day of the week for a Jew like Paul was Sunday. He urged the Christians at Corinth not to wait until he arrived and then scramble to take an offering. Instead, he suggested that they save a little each week as they may prosper. Tithing (giving ten percent of your income) should be the lower limit for a Christian, not the required standard. Paul says in this verse that our gifts should be as the Lord blesses us. If He blesses us exceedingly, our giving should reflect that. Some folks assume that the more the Lord blesses, the more they have to spend. It might be equally true that the Lord is blessing you so you will have more to give.

The Bible clearly speaks to the need of giving. In the Book of Haggai, God takes the people to task because they were not giving to help rebuild the temple. He warns them of the consequences of their miserliness:

> Then the word of the LORD came by Haggai the prophet, saying, "Is it time for you yourselves to dwell in your paneled houses, and this temple to lie in ruins?" Now therefore, thus says the LORD of hosts: "Consider your ways! You have sown much, and bring in little; you eat, but do not have enough; you drink, but you are not filled with drink; you clothe yourselves, but no one is warm; and he who earns wages, earns wages to put into a bag with holes" (Haggai 1:3–6).

If you have a lot of month left after your paycheck is gone, not only do you have to ask, "How much am I earning and how much am I spending?" but also, "How much am I giving?" God can make 90 percent stretch farther than you can stretch 100 percent.

You may think, *These are all Old Testament verses. I live in New Testament times. I live under grace, not law.* But 2 Timothy 3:16–17 says, "All Scripture is given by inspiration of God, and is profitable for doctrine, for reproof, for correction, for instruction in righteousness, that the man of God may be complete, thoroughly equipped for every good work." That *all* includes the Old Testament. God's methods may change (we give now in response to grace, not law), but His principles remain

117

the same. You become equipped for living by following all of God's principles. The New American Standard version translates the word *equipped* as "adequate." You become an adequate provider as you trust the Lord with your finances.

Finally, beware of the debt trap. A study done by Brown University discovered that financial problems are a major cause of divorce in 80 percent of couples under the age of thirty. Even if it doesn't lead to divorce, debt becomes a bone of contention for many married couples.

One of the most common ways people, including Christians, get themselves head over heels in debt is through credit cards. In 1996 the average household had four credit cards with balances of around $4,800. Making the minimum payment on a $4,800 balance at the average annual interest rate of 17 percent (and some credit cards have a 21 percent interest rate or higher), it would take thirty-nine years and seven months to pay off. In the meantime, the cardholder would pay $10,818.63 in interest alone. On the average, a credit card purchase will end up costing 112 percent more than a purchase made by cash.[6]

Credit cards can be an easy convenience and a wonderful way to "manage" your money. But if you choose to go this route, you must pay off your balance each time and never carry it to the next month. The first time you get a credit card bill you can't pay off, you should cut up the card, return it to the company it came from, and request that they mail you no more.

For the debt you already have, you might want to look into a debt consolidation loan. The interest on these loans is usually much less than what you're paying on the credit card. Always remember, however, that this type of loan doesn't eliminate your debt; it only consolidates it. This doesn't give you the freedom to go out and get deeper in debt. Use the extra money you free up to pay off your loan early and save even more interest expenses.

Another possibility is to use your savings to pay off your card debt. Compare the interest rate on your savings account with the interest rate you are paying on your credit card. If there is a significant difference, it might be worth doing.

Someone observed tongue in cheek that we live in a marvelous country. You can walk out of your home that's mortgaged to the hilt, get into your car that you are still making payments on, and use credit card gas to drive down a highway built by bonds to charge something at your favorite store. Is that really so marvelous?

One of my friends went to seminary right out of college. All his funds were exhausted by undergraduate expenses, so he thought the only way he could pay his way through seminary was by taking out government loans (they were called Student Defense Loans back then). After two years he decided if the Lord wanted him in school, He could provide without having him go deeply in debt. Five years and two degrees later, God had provided as abundantly as the first two years but without any debt.

Not only does it make good financial sense to get out of debt, but borrowing of any kind can circumvent God's will for your life. God often uses finances as a tool to guide you. If money is not available for something you desire and it does not appear it will be available in the near future, God is probably trying to communicate one of three truths: 1) this is not His will for your life; 2) this is His will but not right now; or 3) this is His will but He has another way to provide.

I know the difficulty of waiting, especially if you only have to take out a piece of plastic or sign a note and you could have what you want now. God, however, is concerned about building your character, not your estate. The wise use of finances teaches you to be patient, to set priorities, and to seek His will. God promises to provide all you need (Philippians 4:19), not all you want.

Be prepared but not dependent

As you look toward the future, there is nothing wrong with making financial preparations. When I was a little boy, I had a Sunday school teacher who use to say, "Live as though the Lord were coming today; plan as though He isn't coming for a hundred years." I believe that the Lord is coming soon, but as the primary provider in the home, I have to plan as though He will tarry for a long time yet.

Many people have done little or no planning for the future. The Social Security Administration reports that 75 percent of retirees depend on friends, relatives, or Social Security as their only source of support. Twenty-five percent of persons over age sixty-five must continue to work out of economic necessity. The LIAMA Cooperative Research says that 93 percent of men age sixty-five who have failed financially claim it was because of the lack of a definite plan.[7]

If you have made little or no plans for the support of your family in case of death or retirement, you are neglecting your responsibility as the provider in the home. You may want to talk to your pastor or ask for the name of a Christian financial planner. I strongly recommend you seek the counsel of a financial planner who is a Christian, because he or she will understand about the need of providing for God's work in the future as well as for your family. Even when you die, your finances can continue to further the work of Christ on earth if you plan properly.

The caution I give is not to become dependent on your plans. Many people are looking toward Social Security to meet a large chunk of their retirement needs. But you have no guarantees that the Social Security system will not go bankrupt. Even should it still be in place when you retire, it was intended to be a safety net, not a replacement for your income.

Bad investments, company downsizing, and corporate failures are leaving numerous people with no private retirement funds at all. The escalating cost of everything from housing to groceries has forced others who thought they had adequate funds for a comfortable retirement either to quit work later than intended or downscale their retirement plans.

The ultimate security for the future, however, does not lie in retirement plans or Social Security but in God. Martin Luther said, "I have tried to keep things in my own hands, and I have lost them all, but what I have given into God's hands I still possess." Jesus said, "Do not lay up for yourselves treasures on earth, where moth and rust destroy and where thieves break in and steal; but lay up for yourselves treasures in heaven, where neither moth nor rust destroys and where thieves do not break in and steal" (Matthew 6:19–20).

THE GOOD PROVIDER

The Bible uses many word pictures to describe the husband and father who is a good provider in the home. He possesses the industry of the ant (Proverbs 6:6), the quiet confidence of the lily (Matthew 6:28), and the planning and foresight of the wise steward (24:45–46). He is the provider in his home, giving leadership, guidance, and strength. But he is also the provider of all his family's material needs.

There are, of course, circumstances that may prohibit you from being the provider in your home—injury, disability, etc. And in our two-income-family society, you may not be the only provider in the home. But it is God's design that you be the primary provider and that you provide as best you can for your family. Not to provide for your family fails both those you love and the God who loves you. Being the provider in the home doesn't mean you shower your children with their every whimsical desire, but it does mean that you plan and prepare to meet all their physical needs, both now and in the future.

Such a person is like a young man who applied for a job as a farmhand. His potential employer asked him what qualifications he might have for the position. The man replied, "I can sleep when the wind blows." That was a curious qualification, but the farmer liked the looks of the boy so he hired him anyway. A few months later, a storm came up in the middle of the night. The farmer was awakened, so he went out to check on things. He found the shutters on the house fastened, a supply of logs brought in for the fireplace, the farm implements in the storage shed, the tractor in the garage—in short, everything had been taken care of. Then it dawned on the farmer what the young man had meant. Because the farmhand had been faithful to perform his work when the skies were clear, he could sleep when the storm broke.

Now is the time to provide for your family. As you care for their current needs and prepare for their future needs, God will bless. And you, too, can sleep when the wind blows.

[1] Ed Hall, U.S. National Debt Clock (http://www.brillg.com/debt_clock).

[2] "Here's Some Disturbing Statistics about Consumer Debt" (http://www.easydebtreduction.com/statistics.html).

[3] Michelle Green, "Fate's Captive," *People Weekly*, December 5, 1988, p. 6.

[4] "The Flick Family Fight," *Newsweek*, September 25, 1972, p. 95.

[5] Mary Beth Schultheis and John Webster, "USDA Report Estimates Child Born in 1999 Will Cost $160,140 to Raise" (http://www.usda.gov/news/releases/2000/04/0138).

[6] Cindy Hall and Sam Ward, "Credit Cards Get Heavier," *USA Today*, June 1, 1994, p. A-1.

[7] Marshall Albarelli, "What Happens When Thirty-Something Becomes Sixty-Something," Lenox Inn, October 21, 1993.

Chapter 8

THE COUNSELOR IN HIS HOME

According to statistics at college counseling centers nationwide, twice as many females seek counseling help as males.[1] Many men claim they have no need for counselors. "Real" men are invincible. They don't cry and they don't ask for help. Men tend to believe only wimps seek assistance from others. The Book of Proverbs, to the contrary, says it is the wise who seek counsel. "Listen to counsel and receive instruction, that you may be wise in your latter days" (19:20).

Perhaps men's reluctance to receive counsel is part of the reason they have a difficult time giving it. Men are good at giving advice but poor at giving counsel. They are not the same. Advice focuses on the problem. Counsel focuses on the person. Advice is geared toward fixing a dilemma. Counsel seeks to understand why there is a dilemma before it gets fixed. Advice takes only a few minutes. Counsel can stretch over a period of months or even years.

An old riddle asks, "What is it that everyone wants to give but no one wants to take?" The answer is advice. People don't want to be "problems" that need to be fixed. They want to be human beings who are more than the sum total of their troubles. That's why the man of the house also needs to be a wise counselor.

Certain dads cringe when they encounter a situation that requires counseling rather than a quick fix of advice. Some think, *I can't counsel. I don't have any training*. A study frequently quoted in beginning psychology courses pitted a group of lay counselors against a group of trained psychologists. The lay counselors were instructed basically to listen to the counselee and not offer a lot of direction. The psychologists were allowed to ply their trade however they saw fit. The results showed that the recovery rate among the two groups of counselees was almost the same.

People (including those who make up our families) are looking for individuals who will listen to them and empathize with them before they offer any solutions. That doesn't require a Ph.D. Any husband and father can listen.

God's Word lays the obligation of being a counselor squarely at the parent's doorstep. Proverbs 1:8 commands, "My son, hear the instruction of your father, and do not forsake the law of your mother." Obviously there are some things that only a mother can offer counsel for, especially to her daughters. In other areas, however, the father is the best counselor his family could hope for, even if he has never had any training.

LAYING THE FOUNDATION

Before you begin to give counsel, you need to demonstrate that you can receive counsel. Don't pretend to have all the answers. That's a dangerous pedestal on which to perch, because sooner or later you will get knocked off. When children see that their father is open to instruction, they are more likely to respond positively when the same need arises for them. Godly men who want to build a godly home are willing to admit their need to know and to learn from others. Someone has said, "Only those willing to be led are fit to lead." The same holds true of counselors.

Counselors in the home need to know where to turn for counsel themselves. Naturally the first place is God's Word. Every problem you may encounter can be answered through a principle from the Scriptures. Jesus promised, "When He, the Spirit of truth, has come, He will guide you into all truth; for He will not speak on His own authority, but whatever He hears He will speak; and He will tell you things to come" (John 16:13). Prayer, the Holy Spirit, and an open Bible can deal with any challenge.

That doesn't mean, however, that we can always discern the answer. The potential is there, but we don't always live up to our potential. That's why God has placed us in a local church. More than once I have been sitting in church when God spoke to me about an area of concern in my life through a hymn, a prayer, or the pastor's message. Nobody knew about my need when they selected that hymn, prayed that prayer, or prepared that message, but the Holy Spirit did. Likely you have had the same experience.

When you receive what you believe is the scriptural principle for your quandary, it is still wise to confirm it in a number of ways. I read recently of a woman who invested her life savings in a deal that turned out to be a sham. She then went to the Better Business Bureau. The man at the desk asked, "You knew we were here. Why didn't you check with us before you invested?" "Well," she admitted, "I was afraid you'd tell me I shouldn't."

Our personal desires sometimes shade what we believe is God's leading. Begin by asking yourself, "Does this 'answer' contradict an obvious teaching of the Bible?" Rest assured, God will never provide an answer to your situation that in any way negates His Word or His revealed will. Don't fool yourself into thinking that you are an exception. There should be a peace in your heart that confirms what you are planning is consistent with what God teaches.

You then need to verify this further through the counsel of a few godly Christians. Choose people whom you respect, people of spiritual maturity and demonstrated wisdom. They may be your pastor or Bible study group leader. A good friend may not be your best choice; he may be too close to you to be objective. Also, be sure you don't select only those who see things the same way you do.

In 1 Kings 22, Jehoshaphat, king of Judah, went down to Ahab, king of Israel. Ahab encouraged him to join together in a war against Syria, and he called together four hundred prophets (apparently prophets of Baal). All of them predicted victory for the kings. Yet Jehoshaphat asked, "Is there not still a prophet of the LORD here, that we may inquire of Him?" The Bible then records, "So the king of Israel said to Jehoshaphat, 'There is still one man, Micaiah the son of Imlah, by whom we may inquire of the LORD; but I hate him, because he does not prophesy good concerning me, but evil'" (22:7–8).

It is difficult to seek the counsel of people who have a different viewpoint than our own. Because of the burden God has placed on their heart, they may not have the same enthusiasm for a project as we have. But for that reason, their understanding may be less biased. It was in the case of Ahab and Jehoshaphat. Micaiah said, "I saw all Israel scattered on the mountains, as sheep that have no shepherd. And the LORD said, 'These have no master. Let each return to his house in peace.' And the king of Israel said to Jehoshaphat, 'Did I not tell you he would not prophesy good concerning me, but evil?'" (vv. 17–18).

Ahab didn't want the truth; he wanted someone who would agree with him. Unfortunately for Ahab and Jehoshaphat, Micaiah was right. They lost the battle and Ahab was killed. Don't surround yourself with yes-men. Listen to the opposition. Sometimes they're the only ones who will tell you the truth.

If your conclusion is consistent with Scripture, if the Holy Spirit gives you a peace in your heart, and if the counsel from godly people is positive, chances are you're on the right track. If, on the other hand, these counsels do not agree, wait and seek the Lord further. He might be saying, "No," or, "Not yet." In either case it would be foolish to rush ahead.

THE PURPOSE OF COUNSELING

When you counsel with those in your family, finding a solution to the issue is not your only goal. As the counselor in your home, you need to train your children how to make wise choices based on God's Word.

They've already seen you search the Scriptures, so you have set a good precedent. But they also need to know how to use God's Word. It's back to the old question, do we give them a fish or a fishing pole? If we pull out all the answers from the Bible for them, we've satisfied their need for right now. If we teach them how to find the answers for themselves, we've prepared them for when we won't be around.

Teach your children how to study the Bible. My study of the Bible often has followed what some call the "Three-Step Method." It consists of three questions I ask of any passage of Scripture: What does the passage say? What does the passage mean? What does the passage mean to me? Let's use the passage in 1 Kings 22 as a sample of this kind of questioning.

What does the passage say? This question asks us simply to state what we know from the text. For example, these verses tells us that Ahab and Jehoshaphat came together to plot war against Syria. They accepted the counsel given them by the false prophets of Baal. In the ensuing battle, their armies were defeated and Ahab was killed.

What does it mean? This question can be rephrased, "Why did God have this event recorded in the Bible?" God always has a reason for everything written in Scripture. In this case these verses show the foolishness of seeking God's will from those who don't know Him. They also demonstrate the wisdom of accepting godly counsel even when it goes against what we want to hear.

What does it mean to me? This question focuses on application. We could say that these verses teach us to seek godly men and women to help us discern God's will for our lives. It also implies that we need to listen to them even if we don't like what we hear.

When we train our children to make wise choices based on the Bible, we won't always have to look over their shoulder. We can be confident that they will come to conclusions that honor the Lord because they will know how to read, understand, and apply His Word.

AREAS OF CONCERN

As children grow up, they face many decisions. As the counselor in the home, you need to begin early to teach them how to make godly decisions concerning various areas in their lives. Some of the more difficult decisions relate to the following.

Friends

One of the first decisions they must make concerns their choice of friends. Even before they go to school, most children develop friendships. If your child can't read, you can still share and discuss with him what the Bible says about friends. Using a children's Bible or one that will be understandable to him, read Proverbs 1:10–16:

> My son, if sinners entice you, do not consent. If they say, "Come with us, let us lie in wait to shed blood; let us lurk secretly for the innocent without cause; let us swallow them alive like Sheol, and whole, like those who go down to the Pit; we shall find all kinds of precious possessions, we shall fill our houses with spoil; cast in your lot among us, let us all have one purse"—my son, do not walk in the way with them, keep your foot from their path; for their feet run to evil, and they make haste to shed blood.

This passage urges young people to stay away from those who will lead them into trouble. Today's friends are the source of tomorrow's peer pressure. When children reach early adolescence (usually beginning in junior high), the center of their concerns shifts from family to peers. They face such an urge to belong, to fit in, that frequently they will go along with the group even when it means doing things they know their parents wouldn't approve of.

In the spring of 1993, Lakewood, California, a middle-class suburb of Los Angeles, received national attention over a sex scandal involving teenage peer pressure. The public learned that some of the most popular boys at Lakewood High School had formed a sexual-conquest group (the "Spur Posse") in which they scored a point every time they had sexual relationships with a girl. Some of these girls were as young as ten.

When questioned, the girls said they felt pressured into having sex with the boys in order to be accepted.

Your children are too precious for you to allow them to get involved in such destructive activities. Counsel them from God's Word that no matter what enticement these "friends" offer, they will get caught sooner or later. Proverbs 1:18–19 says, "But they lie in wait for their own blood, they lurk secretly for their own lives. So are the ways of everyone who is greedy for gain; it takes away the life of its owners." Pray that your children will discern at a young age that those who practice evil are not real friends and that every behavior has consequences.

The counselor in the home also needs to teach his children to look for friends who have a wise heart and not a wise mouth. Proverbs 15:5 and 7 declare, "A fool despises his father's instruction, but he who receives correction is prudent. . . . The lips of the wise disperse knowledge, but the heart of the fool does not do so." Jesus said, "But those things which proceed out of the mouth come from the heart, and they defile a man. For out of the heart proceed evil thoughts, murders, adulteries, fornication, thefts, false witness, blasphemies" (Matthew 15:18–19).

In other words, a foolish mouth indicates a foolish heart. Frankly, our children don't need friends who will encourage them to be foolish. They can do that well enough on their own.

Furthermore, a child needs to be counseled to look for friends who will build him up rather than tear him down. Proverbs 16:27–28 says, "An ungodly man digs up evil, and it is on his lips like a burning fire. A perverse man sows strife, and a whisperer separates the best of friends." Samuel Butler, the English satirist, said, "Friendship is like money—easier made than kept." Our children don't need friends who are whisperers, liars, tale tellers, or gossipers. As Butler implies, relationships are challenging enough without pseudo friends adding these problems.

And one final word about friends. You need to teach your family about the dangers of taking up with moochers. We've all encountered moochers before. A moocher is a person who wants something from you but doesn't give anything back. Proverbs 19:4 reminds us, "Wealth makes many friends, but the poor is separated from his friend." This advice is especially important if your children are sensitive and compassionate. I have a daughter who is tenderhearted. She will readily take people anywhere or do anything for them. As a consequence, she's easily taken advantage of. You want your children to be kind and generous, but you must teach them the difference between generosity and gullibility. Through God's Word, remind them that moochers don't make good friends.

Higher education

When your children get into high school, they probably will begin to think about the possibility of higher education. The important question is, what does the Lord want?

Not everyone is cut out for a college or university education, and that's fine. God needs Christians in the trades both here and overseas. Opportunities abound for mechanics, bookkeepers, computer technicians, and administrative personnel. It's not the degree that counts; it's God's call on your life.

But God does call some of our children to a more academic undertaking. That means choices need to be made among a myriad of colleges and universities. I still remember those late-night sessions with my children when we spread college catalogs all over the kitchen table. We read about the institution's history and looked at both the academic and social life of the college. If it was a Christian college, we read the statement of faith carefully and discussed it. Most of all, we prayed. Oh, how we prayed!

I also recommend that you help your children narrow their choices to just a few and then visit the colleges personally. While you're on campus, visit some of the places where students gather. Listen to what they say about the faculty, the courses, and campus life in general. Uncensored conversations offer the best opportunity to get true insight into the philosophy of the school. Slick view books and professional videos are the least reliable sources of information. If you want to know the real story, ask the students themselves.

In addition to the current students, make contact with some of the alumni. Ask them how the college compares now to when they attended. If there has been a liberal drift, they will quickly tell you.

Also, check out the theology of the college closely. Find out what role the Bible plays in the curriculum. Now you may say, "Wait a minute. My kids are going to a state university. It doesn't have a theology, and the Bible doesn't play any role in the curriculum." Keep in mind that whichever college or university your child attends, he or she will receive more than an academic education. If learning were only a matter of imparting facts, it wouldn't matter for the most part where your child attends—facts are facts. But every education shapes our children's values and lifestyle as well.

Ask yourself, "Am I willing to hand over my treasured child to a professional values shaper whose views are very different from mine?" First-year college students are very vulnerable. During the years I taught at both a Christian university and a Bible college, I found that first-semester freshmen were really only high school students pretending to be college students. They were impressionable and pliable.

Make your college choices based on more than the fact that a particular institution offers programs in your child's area of interest. (The majority of students change their major at least once between entering college and completing their sophomore year anyway.) Finances are not the bottom line either. If God wants your child at a particular college, He'll help you find a way to pay for it.

The Book of Proverbs says that the most important matter in education is obtaining wisdom and understanding. "Get wisdom! Get understanding! Do not forget, nor turn away from the words of my mouth" (4:5). Verse 7 reminds us, "Wisdom is the principal thing; therefore get wisdom. And in all your getting, get understanding." Wisdom and understanding are the consequences of knowing how to apply knowledge so that everyone benefits from it. We have a plague of educated fools in influential positions in the world today. They are a storehouse of knowledge, but they lack the necessary basis for true wisdom. "The fear of the LORD is the beginning of wisdom, and the knowledge of the Holy One is understanding" (9:10). Be careful how you counsel your children in regard to education. Be even more careful with whom you entrust them to be educated.

We want more than an education for our children. The counselor in the home also desires for them to gain a godly wisdom in knowing how to deal with people. A study at Carnegie Institute of Technology showed that only about 15 percent of a person's business and engineering success is due to technical knowledge, and 85 percent is due to "human engineering skills," such as the ability to lead and influence people. Likewise, when people are discharged from their jobs in industry, only 20 to 40 percent are let go because they lack technical skills. Most of them (60 to 80 percent) are fired because they lack human relations skills.[2]

Getting an education is more than learning how to do a job. It involves learning how to live wisely. Children need a father who will show by his godly counsel how important they are to him. Counsel your children not just to learn facts but to learn how to influence people for God and for good. Fathers are the most trusted counselors even if they have not attended college themselves. Don't lose this wonderful opportunity to be the counselor of your home.

Career

Some young people leave high school and move directly into a job. Others choose to receive more education. Sooner or later, however, a choice of careers must be made. Chances are your children will come to you for counsel on choosing their vocation. And they should. After all, you've been in a career for years. This is one area in which you're an expert.

Proverbs 22:6 says, "Train up a child in the way he should go, and when he is old he will not depart from it." We usually think of this verse in the context of spiritual training. Evidence points toward the fact that originally it was used in the context of a trade. "Train up" a child in a particular vocation, and when he is old he will continue on in that trade. Whether we take this instruction spiritually or vocationally, the writer implies a truth important to the counselor in the home. We must start to teach our children when they are young.

We can't choose their career for them, but we do need to begin reminding our children at a young age that they have been bought with a price. Paul declares, "For you were bought at a price; therefore glorify God in your body and in your spirit, which are God's" (1 Corinthians 6:20). Their bodies as well as their spirits belong to God, and He saved them for a purpose. Advise your children not to choose a vocation according to what their interests are or what will make the most money. Remind them of their responsibility to discern God's will for their life. That message needs to be frequently repeated in family conversations, family devotions, and those special occasions when your children question you about careers.

The American Council on Education surveyed two hundred thousand incoming freshmen in 1987. Seventy-five percent said that being well-off financially was either an "essential" or a "very important" goal. Seventy-one percent said that the key reason they were going to college was to make more money when they graduated. Only 39 percent thought it was vital to develop a meaningful philosophy of life. Apparently the parents of these young people failed to counsel them concerning the truth about money.

Life magazine ran a picture of David Kennedy, the son of Robert F. Kennedy, in the June 14, 1968, issue. The picture, which had been snapped by Jacqueline Kennedy, showed him sitting on the White House lawn, gazing out over a pond. The president had inscribed it with these words, "A future president inspects his property." David Kennedy had the wealth and social status to have anything he wanted, but he committed suicide at age twenty-eight.

Money is not the answer. You must both model for your children and counsel them that a career chosen for that reason will never satisfy. Only when we respond to God's call on our lives do we find fulfillment. Help your children hear His call.

Future mate

The Bible has a lot to say about choosing a spouse. As the counselor in the home, you have the unique privilege and awesome responsibility to teach your children these truths long before they begin to date. Standards need to be established from the outset. Once an individual becomes emotionally involved, it's far more difficult to explain and enforce guidelines.

Dating is far more important than it is given credit for. Many girls have said, "I know this boy isn't a Christian, but we're just going on a date—not getting married!" A year later they're married and your son-in-law is still not a Christian. If a fellow is not someone a Christian girl could potentially marry, then he is not someone to date (and this goes for girls as well).

When I counseled my son, Tim, about dating, I read him Proverbs 31:10–11: "Who can find a virtuous wife? For her worth is far above rubies. The heart of her husband safely trusts her; so he will have no lack of gain."

If you planned to buy a new car, you would study what the experts say about various models and consider your personal needs and many other things. The Bible says a good wife is worth far more than rubies—or cars. Why shouldn't you then take the same kind of care when choosing the one you plan to spend your life with?

I counseled my three daughters, Tracy, Tina, and Tiffany, with Proverbs 20:5–7: "Counsel in the heart of man is like deep water, but a man of understanding will draw it out. Most men will proclaim each his own goodness, but who can find a faithful man? The righteous man walks in his integrity; his children are blessed after him."

I always told my daughters that faithfulness is the chief quality to look for in a man. Much of the heartbreak in marriage stems from unfaithfulness. Although the gap is closing, men tend to be unfaithful more often than their wives. Usually it begins innocently enough. A look that lingers a little too long. A touch that conveys more than it should. Some lighthearted flirtations. But from there it grows to become an all-consuming passion.

In 1878 an international company attempted to dig a canal across Panama. It failed. In 1889 a French company headed by the man who built the Suez Canal also tried. It failed.

What was the problem? It wasn't the mountains, though they were formidable. It wasn't the jungle, though it was dense. The real problem was the mosquitoes that carried yellow fever. Until the U.S. Medical Corps wiped out the mosquito in 1905, the project couldn't go on.

As the counselor in the home, you need to teach your sons and daughters that if they will be faithful in the small things of life, the big things will take care of themselves. People don't stumble over mountains; they stumble over molehills. It's the little foxes that spoil the vines.

HEAVENLY REWARDS

The counselor in the home will never earn the big bucks that professional counselors do, but he will have his reward. He will have a direction in his life based on God's principles. He will have a wife and children who know that their husband/father is a source of wisdom when they need help. Most of all, he will have eternal rewards in heaven as he fulfills the command to "train up" those under his authority.

Why do men fail in their role as counselor in the home? Usually because they feel inadequate and unqualified. Any father who draws his counsel from God's Word, however, is eminently qualified to be the counselor in his home. And any father who disregards the Bible is completely unqualified, regardless of his education. Men of God never need to feel inadequate to do what He calls them to do. God is Himself their adequacy. With God, all things are possible, even being a counselor in the home.

[1]"Men Reluctant to Seek Counseling Help," *USA Today* (periodical), December 1992, p. 2.

[2] Keith W. Sehnert, *Stress/Unstress* (Minneapolis: Augsburg, 1981), p. 100.

Chapter 9

THE DISCIPLINARIAN IN HIS HOME

"Children today are tyrants. They contradict their parents, they gobble their food, they terrorize their teachers." Does this sound familiar, as if it were out of today's newspaper? Well, take heart. Socrates said that more than two thousand years ago.

Children haven't really changed. They dress differently, play with Game Boys, and hang out in malls, but underneath they are much like the children of Socrates' day.

Albert Siegel stated in *The Stanford Observer*, "When it comes to rearing children, every society is only twenty years away from barbarism. Twenty years is all we have to accomplish the task of civilizing the infants who are born into our midst each year. These savages know nothing of our language, our culture, our religion, our values, or our customs of interpersonal relations. The infant is totally ignorant about communism, fascism, democracy, civil liberties, the rights of the minority as contrasted with the prerogatives of the majority, respect, decency, honesty, customs, conventions, and manners. The barbarian must be tamed if civilization is to survive."

One of the ways we tame our little "barbarians" is through discipline. Children always have and always will need the firm controlling hand of a father who knows how to discipline them. The old maxim "Spare the rod, spoil the child" is not found in Scripture, but its intent surely is. Proverbs 13:24 says, "He who spares his rod hates his son, but he who loves him disciplines him promptly."

There is much concern these days about discipline because some parents have misunderstood it and therefore have misused it. In fact, a growing number of people in our society are calling for every form of corporal punishment to be outlawed.

Such an extreme position is both unreasonable and illogical. It is unreasonable because when corporal discipline has been abandoned in the past (most recently under the influence of Dr. Benjamin Spock), the result has been chaotic. It is illogical because if that argument were applied across the board, no one could drive because some people—like drunk drivers—misuse their cars. No one would be able to eat because many people abuse their bodies through food. In fact, if we were consistent with this approach, we wouldn't be able to do much of anything. It never works to throw the proverbial baby out with the bath water. But as a Christian and as one who bears the major responsibility for disciplining his household, you need to understand what discipline is and is not.

WHAT IS DISCIPLINE?

Discipline is related to the word *disciple*, one who learns and follows. The goal of discipline, therefore, is to teach and give direction. Children may not always understand or appreciate that truth, but parents must always remember that this is their goal or the results can be catastrophic. Therefore, let's first consider what discipline is not.

Discipline is not punishment

Discipline is based on a concern for the child's future. Punishment is primarily concerned with the present. When we punish, we are trying to get even. Punishment says, "You caused me pain by your behavior, so I'm going to cause you an equal amount of pain." The goal of discipline, on the other hand, is not to pay back a child for his misbehavior; it is to teach with an eye towards the child's future. Discipline says, "You have done something that will harm you or someone else. If you do this when you grow up, people will not accept you. You will have a difficult time making friends and/or keeping a job. I have to teach you not to do this so that you can function in the adult world when the time comes."

One day a vacationer stopped by the studio of a famous potter. Intrigued, he watched the man pound a large lump of clay. Jokingly he asked, "Are you taking out your frustrations, or are you doing something constructive?" "Just watch and see," the potter replied. Soon tiny air bubbles began to appear on the surface of the clay. "I could never shape the clay into a quality pot," the potter explained, "if those pockets of air were not removed."

The disciplinarian is in the process of making a quality pot, a vessel that will be useful and a source of blessing to others for years to come. But the clay has to be carefully prepared. This is the job of discipline.

Discipline flows out of love; punishment finds its origins in anger. The source of the flow taints the stream. In areas where there are strong iron deposits, the water bubbling up is almost red from the rust sediments. In other areas the spring is clear and clean because the defiling deposits are not present. A child intuitively knows when he's being disciplined out of love or punished out of anger and responds accordingly. Anger breeds anger, while love eventually results in appreciation.

If you look back on your school years, you remember in appreciation those teachers who cared enough to discipline you to study. You may not have esteemed them at the time, but now you see the value in establishing the parameters that enable you to learn. In contrast, those who were simply trying to bully you into submission so they could get on about their business still bring back feelings of resentment.

Discipline shapes the child's will, while punishment breaks the spirit. Every child is born with a strong will—some stronger than others.

In his book *The Strong-Willed Child*, Dr. James Dobson makes the point that some children are born smoking a stogie and shaking their fist, while others are more naturally compliant. Nevertheless, all children have their moments when they are determined not to budge and you aren't going to make them. Discipline rechannels that strong will into areas that can profit from its strength. It's like redirecting a river so that it flows life-giving water through a desert.

Punishment, on the other hand, doesn't rechannel this energy anywhere. Its desire is to control, not train. As a consequence, the spirit shrivels up and dies because it sees no future.

Discipline is not abuse

One of the most valuable concepts I have learned is that truth is like a circle rather than a straight line. If it were a straight line, then the farther we would go in the appropriate direction, the more right we would become. If truth is a circle, however, any extreme we follow—right, left, up, or down—would take us out of that circle of truth.

Abuse is discipline taken out of the circle of truth. When practiced in the extreme, even well-intentioned discipline becomes unintentional abuse. It is heartbreaking to see the amount of abuse in our society today. Parents who were abused as children themselves are inflicting horrendous torture on their own youngsters, who cannot defend themselves.

I define physical abuse by this acronym: ABUSE is **A**lways **B**eating **U**p on **S**omeone **E**lse. There are as many ways to abuse people as there are people. Abuse can occur against either gender, at any age, in any place. Here we are concerned with child abuse, and like all abuse, child abuse takes a variety of forms.

Physical abuse ranges from burning a child with the lighted ends of cigarettes, to locking him in a closet, to breaking bones, and even to death itself. A mother in Baltimore flicked a lighted cigarette into a bedroom closet. She then left her two daughters, Christina, four, and Natalie, two, to perish in the flames. A young mother in Nebraska was sentenced to prison for, among other things, locking her eight-year-old son in a small pet kennel in their basement overnight. No one can read stories like these without feeling a pang of grief for these innocent lives.

Neglect is another form of abuse. A research project at the University of Illinois involved calling two thousand homes at random between the hours of midnight and 2 A.M. on a Friday night in Chicago. The purpose was to see how many parents knew where their children were at that time. To their surprise, the researchers discovered that three-fourths of the calls were answered by a child who did not know where his parents were.[1]

Physical abuse is the kind we usually see on TV or read about in the newspaper. Bruises, lacerations, and dislocated shoulders are among its evidences. But there is another kind of abuse that isn't so obvious. It doesn't leave scars on the flesh but on the soul. This abuse takes the form of screaming and calling kids names like "stupid," "lazy," and "ugly."

A child will believe what he hears no matter how unreasonable it might be. Dr. David Seamands, a Christian psychologist, notes, "Children are the world's greatest recorders, but they are the world's worst interpreters."[2] Kids pick up these condemnations and grow into adulthood believing the lies they were told. They spend their lives either trying to prove they aren't what others claimed they were or simply giving up in defeat.

Another abuse found too often in our society concerns the illicit relationships between parents and children or between siblings themselves. Katherine Edwards (not her real name) was one of those victims. Her adoptive father sexually abused her from the time she was in sixth grade through junior high. He threatened and bullied his teenage daughter to keep quiet about his sin. All during this time, her father was a respected member of the church and the community. "The effects on my life were devastating," Katherine says.[3]

Punishment and abuse are common, but they are not discipline. Discipline leaves a child better prepared to function as an adult. Punishment and abuse destroy a child's self-worth and leave him feeling like a damaged piece of merchandise. The degree of damage may vary from child to child, and God is able to heal someone from abuse. Still, it should be the aim of every Christian to rid our society of abusive extremes while maintaining a discipline that produces end results pleasing to God.

If you are to accomplish this goal, you will need a standard of truth that never changes, a source of counsel that never fails, and a set of principles that will guide you as the disciplinarian in the home. In short, when it comes to discipline you need to turn back to the Bible.

BIBLICAL TRUTHS

Despite cries to the contrary, a lack of discipline is not a sign of love. The parent who says, "Oh, I just love Junior too much to discipline him," doesn't understand either love or discipline. Discipline is tough. It puts stress on your relationship with your child. Obviously, your son or daughter will not like it. Hebrews 12:11 admits, "Now no chastening seems to be joyful for the present, but grievous . . . to those who have been trained by it." Rarely is discipline appreciated when it is meted out.

Furthermore, discipline drains you emotionally. There are times when you're so tired you would rather overlook a transgression than deal with it. Other times the pain of administering the discipline is just as strong for you as it is for your child. Neither the giver nor the receiver looks forward to discipline. This responsibility is definitely not for the faint-hearted.

It takes a deep love and a strong commitment to the future welfare of your child to suffer the negative consequences of being the disciplinarian in the home. Love doesn't say, "Let the child do anything he wants." Love says, "I must discipline my child so that when he grows up, he won't make mistakes that will alienate him from others. He will know how to function as an adult because I taught him."

BIBLICAL EXAMPLES

Only one thing is more painful than disciplining your child—living with the regret that you didn't. Several Bible characters learned that lesson the hard way.

I have chosen three examples from the Bible of fathers who failed to discipline their sons. I chose these for your encouragement. Eli, Samuel, and David aren't nobodies. They were "stars" of ancient Israel. If men of this caliber can make mistakes in disciplining their children, we are not above the same blunders. Take heart that even kings and priests aren't experts at disciplining.

Eli

Eli was a judge over Israel for forty years and served as a priest at Shiloh. Hannah met Eli while she was praying for a son and found comfort in his encouragement. When her son, Samuel, was born, she dedicated him to serve with Eli at the tabernacle.

Eli apparently did a good job raising Samuel but failed as a father to his own sons, Hophni and Phinehas. These young men were disrespectful and immoral. Their sexual exploits displayed the highest degree of brashness and insensitivity. Yet Scripture never mentions that Eli disciplined them. All we read is Eli's plaintive complaint, "Why do you do these things? For I hear of your evil dealings from all the people" (1 Samuel 2:23).

Eli admonished his boys but never disciplined them. Children quickly learn whether it's safe to ignore a parent or not. If words are the worst they receive, most will do what they want. That's what Eli's sons chose to do, and as a result of their sin God allowed them to be killed in battle.

When the elderly Eli heard the tragic news, he fell off his stool and broke his neck—a sad ending to a great man. Yet many parents have had their hearts—if not their necks—broken because they refused to seriously discipline their children. Talk is never so cheap as when it becomes a substitute for serious discipline. But in the long run, nothing is more costly.

Samuel

Having been dedicated to the service of God by his mother, Samuel grew up in the priest's home. He watched Eli's failure to properly discipline Hophni and Phinehas. You would think after what Samuel saw happen, he would have been a strong disciplinarian. Evidently that was not the case.

Often a minister of the Gospel forgets that he is also the father of a child. Apparently this is what happened to Samuel. The balance between family and ministry is a delicate one. We must earnestly consider Jesus' admonition to place the highest priority on our calling from God (Luke 14:26) without abandoning our call to fatherhood (1 Timothy 5:8). Both Eli and Samuel took God's call to ministry seriously but failed to devote enough attention to being the father their children needed.

When it came time for Samuel to retire (1 Samuel 8), the people came to him and said, "We don't want your sons to reign over us." Evidently they had a legitimate complaint. Scripture says, "But his sons did not walk in his ways; they turned aside after dishonest gain, took bribes, and perverted justice" (v. 3). They were young men whose judgments were based on the highest bidder.

Samuel was a great judge and a godly prophet, but he flunked fathering.

David

David is our third outstanding Bible character who failed fatherhood. He enjoyed significant victories over the Philistines and other nations. He extended the empire farther than it had ever been. David was even called a man after God's own heart (Acts 13:22). But he didn't know how to discipline his children.

Second Samuel 13 tells the sordid story of Amnon, King David's son by Ahinoam the Jezreelitess. Amnon forced himself upon his half-sister, Tamar, the daughter of David and Maachah. This is terrible enough, but verse 21 says, "But when King David heard of all these things, he was very angry." That's it! Period! He let his anger show; perhaps he even yelled a little. But David never translated his negative emotions into positive actions. He didn't lift a finger to discipline his son.

The consequences were disastrous for both David and his children. What began as incest turned into fratricide (Absalom, Tamar's brother, killed Amnon in revenge) and insurrection (Absalom attempted to overthrow King David, his father). Lives were lost or ruined because David let slide his responsibility to be the disciplinarian in his home. The actions of Amnon and Absalom betray David's shortcomings as a father.

HOW TO DISCIPLINE

It's as evident from the Bible characters we've looked at as it is from the evening news that a lack of discipline leads to disastrous results. Having seen the tragic end of not properly disciplining our children, let's consider some dos and don'ts of discipline.

The don'ts

I mention the don'ts first because they are more common. In fact, what this book calls don'ts, most people practice as dos. Here are some of the don'ts of discipline.

Don't discipline in anger. Anger is most often a factor in abuse—both verbal and physical. We say someone who is angry is "mad." That assessment is closer to the truth than we realize. To be mad means to be out of control, to be out of touch with reality. When we are angry, we are not in control of ourselves. We say and do things that we regret later.

Lawrence J. Peter said, "Speak when you're angry—and you'll make the best speech you'll ever regret." Anger brings hurtful words to our lips. Once there, those words are spoken and we can never retract them. We may apologize. We may ask forgiveness. But the damage is already done.

Some of these angry words and deeds will be remembered long after the cause for such a display is forgotten. I once sat in a circle of church leaders who were sharing some of their experiences. One elderly man spoke with a choked voice about some things that had been said and done in a church dispute. He was obviously pained—and these experiences had taken place forty years earlier.

It can happen in a church family; it can happen in your family. The English poetess Elizabeth Barrett Browning was married to Robert Browning in 1846. Her father bitterly opposed the marriage. The Brownings moved to Italy, where they lived out their lives, but Elizabeth wrote her parents almost weekly. After ten years she received a large box in the mail. Inside was a decade's worth of unopened correspondence. The gall of bitterness deprived the whole family of tremendous blessings.

In their anger, people become unreasonable. They lose their ability to think logically. As the disciplinarian in your home, don't let an uncontrolled temper cause you to do or say something you may regret for the rest of your life.

Don't use your hand. This may seem insignificant but it's not. Hands are very important in Scripture. They convey approval and acceptance. The apostle Paul said that when he and Barnabas came to Jerusalem to meet with the disciples, they were given the "right hand of fellowship" (Galatians 2:9). This exchange of handshakes indicated that James,

Peter, and John, the pillars of the Jerusalem church, approved of the ministry to the Gentiles and that Paul and Barnabas were accepted as fellow ministers.

Hands also can be the channels for blessing. Paul admonished Timothy, his son in the faith, "Therefore I remind you to stir up the gift of God which is in you through the laying on of my hands" (2 Timothy 1:6). Paul passed on to Timothy a special gift that needed to be exercised. The conveyance of this gift was symbolized by the laying on of hands.

Furthermore, hands can bring healing. The Gospel of Mark relates one of several times in which Jesus healed a leper. Mark 1:41 says, "And Jesus, moved with compassion, put out His hand and touched him, and said to him, 'I am willing; be cleansed.'" Healing could have taken place without the touch. The Bible records instances where Jesus even healed from a distance. Yet there was more than one kind of healing taking place in this account.

Leprosy caused a person to become unclean, untouchable. For years this man had been forced to warn everyone away by shouting, "Unclean! Unclean!" Jesus wanted to bring more than physical healing to him; He also wanted to heal him emotionally. For the first time in years, this leper felt a human touch. There was an outer healing of the leprosy, but equally important, an inner healing took place as well.

We may not be able to heal a physical disease, but a touch of our hands can meet some important internal needs. Allison Bell, author of the article "The Affection Connection," says, "Touching can soothe you when you're upset, warm you up when you're cold and make you feel better almost immediately."[4]

Dr. Marilyn Ruman, a clinical psychologist in private practice in Encino, California, claims, "To touch and to be touched is one of the most essential needs of human beings."[5]

We never outgrow this need. Infants need it. In fact, they will experience serious consequences if they don't receive it. In 1915 pediatrician Henry Dwight Chapin undertook a study of orphanages in ten American cities. These institutions provided their infants with the basic care needed for survival. They were fed and their diapers were changed, but because of staff limitations, the babies were not held or played with. Dr. Chapin discovered that every child under the age of two died. Probable cause: a lack of personal touch.[6]

Adolescents need a loving touch also. Tracy, a fifteen-year-old, says she'll never give up her after-dinner walks with her father because during those walks he often links arms with her.

Numerous studies report links between promiscuity and the amount of appropriate touching between fathers and adolescent daughters. If a girl does not receive these outward demonstrations of affection at home, she will seek it elsewhere. This leads her into relationships with other males that are neither moral nor emotionally healthy.

Adults need proper physical contact too. Dr. James Lynch, director of the Lifecare Health Institute in Baltimore, Maryland, has observed that touching can lower a person's heart rate and blood pressure. "For example," he says, "when a nurse holds a patient's hand, we've seen significant changes in that patient's heart rate and rhythm. What we're seeing is that we humans can actually reach out and touch each other's heart." [7]

Therefore, the hand is an inappropriate object to use for discipline. When something causes pain, that object becomes connected to the discomfort it causes. If you use your hand to discipline, your children will associate it with fear and pain instead of acceptance, blessing, and healing. Let the negative emotions be connected with a spoon or a paddle or other such object instead.

Don't discipline above the belt. The body is an amazing creation. I was engrossed as I read Dr. Phillip Brand's and Phillip Yancey's book *Fearfully and Wonderfully Made*, which explores the wonders of the body. Like the rest of God's creation, the body is perfectly adapted to our earth's environment. We have muscles where we need them, stretched over a skeletal frame and packaged in a remarkably supple outer wrapping called skin. We also have extra fatty tissue where we need, such as on our sitting end.

It's my firm belief that God put extra padding there to be the ideal place for a swat. Such cushioning exists nowhere else. In fact, using any other part of the body (and this includes pulling hair and twisting ears) can be destructive both physically and emotionally.

Dr. David Seamands talks about counseling people who struggle with deep pain, rage, or hurt. At first they seem oblivious to any cause for such a condition. Frequently he will then ask them, "Tell me, what's the worst picture in all of your memory?"

Before long, he says, their eyes will fill with tears (even big, hulking men) and they will say something like, "Oh, I know what it is. I remember. It was when Dad would lash out and hit me on the head. It was when Mother would slap me." Dr. Seamands goes on to say, "Nothing is more destructive to a human personality than a slap in the face. It is so humiliating, so demeaning, so deeply dehumanizing. It destroys something very basic to our personhood."[8] Every parent should resolve to make any part of the body above the belt off-limits for corporal discipline.

The dos

Real discipline is not just ruling out what you should not do; it's also reaffirming what you should do. Let's now think about the dos of discipline.

Do grow up yourself. You cannot train up a child to be a mature adult (the goal of discipline) unless you yourself are grown up. Perhaps one of the reasons so many children fail to make that transition from childhood to adulthood is because numerous parents never succeeded in finishing that task themselves. Could the person who said that "men never grow up; their toys just get more expensive" be at least partially right?

If you fall victim to uncontrollable rage, undisciplined spending habits, or ungoverned sexual passions, you are in as much need of discipline as your child. I would urge you to talk to your pastor, a Christian counselor, or at least a mature friend who can help you face your problems and, with God's help, conquer them. A man who cannot master himself is in no condition to guide someone else.

Children look to the father in the home to be their example, their rock, their hero. But when a child sees his father living an undisciplined life, how can he respect that man's attempt to discipline him? Discipline yourself before you discipline your children. It will make your role as the disciplinarian in the home much more effective.

Do vary your discipline. Consider reserving corporal punishment (spanking) only for extreme situations, such as outright rebellion. Other options such as time-out, loss of privileges, or extra chores are possibilities, depending on your child's age.

As your son or daughter grows older, other disciplinary measures should take the place of physical discipline. Spanking a teenager is not only humiliating to him but might endanger you. I've seen plenty of six-foot, rock-hard football players who probably could have spanked their fathers.

Since discipline's purpose is to teach a child appropriate behavior, the consequences of misconduct should be associated with the behavior itself. For example, if a child fails to come home in time for supper, he might have to go without any.

When my son was a toddler, he had the habit of wandering out of our yard when he was told not to. His discipline needed to fit his offense. So we confined him to the tub if he wandered. Sitting in the tub fully clothed but not free to roam was just the right form of discipline to teach him to stay in his yard.

Do talk to your child about discipline. As our children grew up we instituted the three-count (when they were younger it was the five-count). We talked about this ahead of time. In fact, we even asked them what they felt an adequate consequence would be for certain types of misbehavior.

Before anything happened, while we were still calm and collected, my wife and I explained that if the culprit did not cease doing (or in some cases, start doing) what we had asked by the time we had slowly counted to three, he or she would suffer the consequence. This seemed the perfect blend between justice and mercy.

By talking about all of this ahead of time, our children knew what they could expect. Furthermore, by setting up the consequences before the event, we were less likely to do anything rash or extreme. One of the most positive outcomes from this effort was that I found myself disciplining less. After the usual tests to find out if I really meant what I said, the kids began to respond before I got to the end of the count.

I must caution you, however, that this form of discipline is unproductive if you do not follow through on the consequences. Few sights are more pathetic than a parent who threatens action against his kids who know he is bluffing or doesn't care enough to follow through with the discipline. If you promise but do not perform, you end up back at square one in embarrassment. Our children need to believe we mean what we say. Without that understanding, discipline is useless.

Do take your turn disciplining. Many a father expects the mother to have everything under control by the time he gets home from work. He becomes upset, then, when it's necessary for him to exercise discipline. The truth of the matter is, rather than gaining more control, most homes deteriorate as the day goes on. Children become tired and cranky in the evenings and therefore require more discipline.

Discipline needs to be administered promptly when the case warrants it, so I don't recommend waiting "until your father gets home." Not only is this a bad way to start the evening for Dad, but too much time may elapse between the event and the consequences. When Dad is home, however, he should be the primary disciplinarian.

As a general rule men are more action-oriented, while women are prone to do more reasoning and cajoling before considering any action. Most of the time discipline calls for action, so Dad is a natural choice.

Ironically, when my wife and I were raising our children, it was just the opposite. I was prone to sit down with my children, probing their misbehavior with a series of questions. We would discuss the whys of their actions and the whys of the consequences. Frequently the children would run to their mother after misbehaving and plead, "Please, Mom, paddle us. Just don't make us listen to one of Dad's lectures." For my children, the real discomfort of discipline was guilt, not physical pain.

WILL THE STATUS BE WEAL OR WOE?

Years ago the Duke of Windsor was quoted by *LOOK* magazine as saying, "The thing that impresses me most about America is the way the parents obey their children." Unfortunately, there's a lot of truth in his observation. Discipline is difficult, so we end up avoiding it by doing whatever the child wants. But it shouldn't be that way.

Any dad who says he enjoys disciplining his children is either a masochist or a liar—or both. Discipline is not fun; it's not supposed to be. But it is necessary, and it is primarily the responsibility of the father in the house.

If you do not discipline your children, it's a sure bet that there is a Hophni, a Phinehas, or an Amnon in your future. Now is the time to take action before matters get out of hand.

If you constantly dump the discipline of your children on your wife, you not only are shirking a divinely appointed responsibility, but you also are being unfair to your wife. It takes two to procreate a child; it also takes two to raise him. Each parent needs to do his or her fair share.

It's time that fathers took up the challenge of being the disciplinarian in the home and change the status quo. If a man is determined to build a godly home, then it's up to him to decide if the situation at home will be weal or woe.

Coupled with the task of discipline is the need for encouragement. A disciplinarian who doesn't know how to encourage will stand a greater chance of breaking his child's spirit and not just his bad habits. The next chapter looks at the role of the encourager in the home.

[1] Dr. David L. Hocking, "What Is a Family?" (tape #7073), Calvary Church, Santa Ana, Calif.

[2] Dr. David Seamands, *Healing for Damaged Emotions* (Wheaton, Ill.: Victor Books, 1984), p. 69.

[3] Stefan Ulstein, "Alone in an Unfriendly World" (a review of *A House Divided: The Secret Betrayal—Incest*), *Christianity Today*, January 1991, p. 34.

[4] Allison Bell, "The Affection Connection," *Teen*, October 1989, p. 20.

[5] Ibid.

[6] Keith W. Sehnert, *Stress/Unstress* (Minneapolis: Augsburg, 1981), p. 101.

[7] Bell, p. 20.

[8] Seamands, p. 42.

Chapter 10

THE ENCOURAGER IN HIS HOME

It's hard to forget those days. We were young and the children we played with were not always kind. Their taunts still ring in our ears: "Sticks and stones may break my bones, but words will never hurt me."

Now that I am an adult and have had some years to reflect on that childish saying, I know how untrue it is. Words can hurt you. In fact, words can scar deeper than silence can ever heal. Proverbs 18:21 says, "Death and life are in the power of the tongue, and those who love it will eat its fruit."

THE POWER OF WORDS

Many people have said that the pen is mightier than the sword, and they are right. Words are some of the most powerful weapons we possess—either for good or evil. They may not break your bones, but they certainly can break your heart.

One of the greatest sermons ever delivered was Jesus' Sermon on the Mount. It can be repeated in five minutes. Lincoln's Gettysburg Address has only ten sentences. It does not take a lot of time or many sentences to make a deep impression; it takes only the right words.

It is estimated that for every word written in Hitler's *Mein Kampf*, 125 people lost their lives in World War II. Don't tell the orphans and widows left behind that words have no power.

A suicide note left by a despondent young woman began, "They said . . . ." She died before she finished the note, but obviously words—untrue, unkind—had motivated her to take her life. You'll never convince her grieving family that words cannot hurt.

What kind of words are spoken in your family? Likely you say they are gentle, positive words. But are you sure? If I asked your wife or your children, would they tell a different story?

A few years ago some parents were asked to participate in an experiment. They were asked to record what they said to their kids and whether they would characterize their remarks as positive or negative. The survey determined that these fathers and mothers spoke critically ten times more often than they spoke favorably toward their children.

Another group was shown a white sheet of paper with a small black dot in the center. Then they were asked what they saw. Everyone replied, "A black dot." The group leader said, "Yes, there is a black dot, but didn't any of you notice the white paper? There's far more of the white paper than there is the black dot."

As fathers we must fight our human tendency to focus on black dots instead of white paper. We have to see all that's right in our family rather than all that's wrong. This may take a serious attitude adjustment on our part.

Negativism is everywhere. It raises its ugly head in domestic quarrels just as it does in political campaigns. It's so easy to choose contrary words instead of confirming words. In one Florida city, teachers were found to be negative 75 percent of the time. When you multiply that by approximately eight hours of class time each day, think of the magnitude of negative input those children received at school. It's little wonder some children hate school. Fortunately, there are many positive teachers who use words to build up their students rather than tear them down.

Some experts claim that it takes four positive statements from an authority figure to offset the effects of one negative statement to a child. If those statistics are correct, fathers have their work cut out for them.

Dad, when God called you to build a godly home, He also appointed you to be its encourager. A Japanese proverb says, "One kind word can warm three winter months." Life becomes cold and discouraging when you are stingy with your encouragement. Life at home becomes unbearable for some teens when they hear nothing but negative comments about them, their friends, their room—everyone and everything in their life.

The famous actress Celeste Holm once said, "We live by encouragement and die without it—slowly, sadly, and angrily."

WHAT IS ENCOURAGEMENT?

The word *encouragement* can be divided into three parts: en-couragement. It's like two small hills with a mountain of courage in the middle. Encouragement means to infuse someone with courage. Put another way, encouragement is the "art of applying love to fear."[1]

Fear comes in all shapes and sizes, but it never comes alone. The late Howard Sugden claimed that every man is haunted by at least two hundred fears. The first emotion mentioned in the Bible is not love or hate, but fear. When Adam was questioned by God after the Fall, he said, "I heard Your voice in the garden, and I was afraid because I was naked; and I hid myself" (Genesis 3:10).

Why is the prevalence of fear such a concern? Because fear is the foundation for discouragement. Perhaps it's the fear of failure, the fear of financial disaster, or the fear of rejection. Whatever its cause, the result of fear is the same—discouragement.

There is a fable about the devil having a garage sale. He prominently displayed some of his tools on a table in order to sell them. They were bright, new, and attractive. Back in a far corner was a much-used and abused old tool. Thinking that this also was for sale, someone picked it up and asked the devil how much he wanted for it. "Oh, no," he said, "that is not for sale. It is one of my favorite tools. I use it often." When asked what this tool was, the devil replied, "Discouragement."

The real danger of discouragement is that it opens the door for all sorts of misery. People have been known to suffer needless illness simply because they were discouraged. What is worse, some have taken their life because they saw no way out. Discouragement is deadly.

On the other hand, when you encourage someone, you help him face his fears. Your loving concern becomes an antidote to the poisonous influence of discouragement. It doesn't mean the one you are helping will no longer be afraid, but he will have the confidence to get through whatever happens.

The Greek word for "encouragement" in the New Testament (*parakaleo*) helps us understand this even better. The word literally means "to call alongside." Encouragement requires two—the one discouraged and an encourager who comes alongside his friend to encourage him. Encouragement always requires the personal involvement of the encourager.

Zig Ziglar tells of an incident in the life of the late Vince Lombardi when he put this into practice. Lombardi was the coach of the Green Bay Packers. During a practice session he noticed one of his big guards was holding out, not putting much of himself into practice. Angrily, Lombardi called the guard aside and laid into him. "Son, you are a lousy football player. You're not blocking, you're not tackling, you're not putting out. As a matter of fact, it's all over for you today. Go take a shower."

The big guard turned and trudged to the locker room. After practice Lombardi walked into the locker room and found the young man, still suited up, quietly sobbing.

Known for being as compassionate as he was volatile, Lombardi went over to the player, put his arm around his shoulders, and said, "Son, I told you the truth. You are a lousy football player. You're not blocking, you're not tackling, you're not putting out. However, in all fairness to you, I should have finished the story. Inside of you, son, there is a great football player, and I'm going to stick by your side until the great football player inside of you has a chance to come out and assert himself."

The player was Jerry Kramer. The commitment Lombardi made to stick by him motivated Kramer to become one of the all-time greats in football. In fact, he was voted the all-time best guard in the first fifty years of the National Football League.

You can't escape fears; they're a part of life. But you need not be destroyed by your fears. That often happens in families where there is no encourager in the home. Your children need your arm around them, Dad. They need someone to spot their fears and stick by them until they work through them.

Fears will come to families, but they can be stopped short of discouragement through the ministry of an encourager. That's one of the ministries of the man of the house.

HOW NOT TO ENCOURAGE

Many well-meaning fathers fumble the ball when it comes to encouragement. They become like Job's friends. When the bottom fell out of Job's life, three of his friends—Eliphaz, Bildad, and Zophar—came to commiserate with him. At first they sat in silence, not opening their mouths. But when they did speak, what they said was no encouragement. They only added to Job's misery.

That can happen to the man of the house too. We don't want to increase someone's pain, of course, but frequently that's what our words do. When trying to be an encourager to your family, you need to make every effort to avoid these common errors.

Quick fix answers. Men don't want to talk about things—they want to fix them. We find out what the problem is and take care of it. Unfortunately, that's not encouraging to most people. In effect it's saying, "Your problem isn't that serious. I can fix it in no time flat."

People do see their problems as serious, or they wouldn't be discouraged about them. When your daughter comes to talk to you about her discouraging social life, she doesn't want a list of fifteen easy steps to successful dating; she wants you to listen and empathize.

It's all right if you can't fix every problem. You aren't Superman. And sometimes it's best if you don't fix right away those things that you can. It may be God's will that they remain broken for a while. In any event, quick fix answers frequently are only a lecture, not encouragement.

Defensive talk. Sometimes we take people's discouragements personally. We become defensive because we somehow feel it's our fault they are discouraged. Whether it is or not, becoming defensive won't help them.

Defensiveness builds walls, not bridges. It insulates you from the people you love the most. The last thing a discouraged son or daughter needs is to be walled out of your life. Instead, they need to be invited in and experience your love and acceptance. The poet Robert Frost talked about his neighbor who said, "Good fences make good neighbors." That may be, but they don't make good encouragers.

Explanations. At times we all need explanations of why things are the way they are. But explanations can be insensitive as well. They are based on logic, whereas discouragement is an emotion. Emotions seldom respond to logic until deeper needs are met.

I once sat with a friend who had just lost his mother. While I was quietly "being there" for my friend, someone came by to say, "I'm so sorry your mother died. But she was so sick. She is better off now. All things work together for good. You'll get along without her. God will help you."

Many of these things were true. My friend's mother was better off in heaven. But these were trite words expressed with little or no meaning. They were something to fill an awkward moment and didn't encourage my friend.

When our friends face the fear that results from having just lost the dearest person on earth to them, they need more than words. They need to know that we will be there for them in their days of discouragement. We will see that their financial needs are met, the snow is shoveled, and the car is repaired. When their fears are met, then they can be comforted by our explanation that their loved one is in heaven.

If explanation alone discourages our friends, imagine what it does to our family. Loved ones need more than an explanation. They need assurance for their fears. Give them yourself.

Lectures. We all know that discouragement is not God's will for our lives. The fear that causes this emotional response indicates we are not trusting God. Remember how many times God encouraged young Joshua as he inherited from Moses the leadership of Israel? "Be strong and of good courage" (Joshua 1:6). "Only be strong and very courageous" (v. 7). "Be strong and of good courage; do not be afraid, nor be dismayed" (v. 9). "Only be strong and of good courage" (v. 18).

Discouragement is like a cancer eating away at our lives. It must be confronted and defeated. But your son, discouraged at his poor academic progress in school, doesn't need to hear your sermon on the sin of discouragement, even if it is well intended. In all likelihood, jumping all over your son for a wrong attitude will only cause him to be defensive and angry, which in turn will lead to more discouragement.

If you're going to build a godly home, you must be an encourager. Discouraged people need a friend, not a critic. They already have plenty of critics. They hurt enough; you don't need to heap more pain on them. You need to help them.

Sarcasm. Sometimes we men struggle with our feelings. When those feelings spill out as sarcasm, we have lost our opportunity to be an encourager.

Suppose your wife has just spent three weeks visiting your new grandchild. She knew she was needed, even if your daughter and son-in-law live in a tiny apartment and had to give up their bed to make room for Grandma. She was having a glorious time doting over that new baby. And what were you doing all this time?

You were still going to work every day, earning a living. In addition you had to cook for yourself, which meant frequent visits to the Golden Arches. You had to clean the house, at least the day your wife returned. You had to do all the things she usually contributes to your family. And while you were doing double duty, what was she doing? Spoiling your grandchild.

When she finally returned home she is depressed. She had to leave the most beautiful baby in the world behind. She is feeling a little empty, a bit discouraged. You say sarcastically, "I hope you had a good time while you left me stranded here at home."

Your remark did little to help her through her depression. You had a wonderful opportunity to be the encourager of the family, but you missed it.

This is not how encouragement works. The husband/father who truly wants to be an encourager to his family finds quick fix answers, insensitive explanations, or sarcasm foreign to his tool kit of encouragement. There is a better way.

HOW TO ENCOURAGE

The writer of Hebrews had some good advice for us. He said, "And let us consider one another in order to stir up love and good works, not forsaking the assembling of ourselves together, as is the manner of some, but exhorting one another, and so much the more as you see the Day approaching" (Hebrews 10:24–25).

The word translated as "exhorting" in verse 25 is again the Greek word *parakaleo*. It's the word that means "to encourage." These verses imply that the ministry of encouragement is not reserved to a special few but can be employed to some extent by every Christian.

In their book *Encouragement: The Key to Caring*, Dr. Larry Crabb and Dan Allender say, "Every Christian, regardless of gift or training, is called upon to encourage his brothers and sisters."[2] You can be an encourager in your home, even without technical training. Let's consider some ways you can make it happen.

Verbal affirmation. Have you noticed that men are not verbal creatures? Your wife probably has. Most men are not good conversationalists. In fact, it is estimated that women speak approximately twenty-five thousand words a day, while men speak about twenty-five hundred. That's a ten to one ratio. Males are more likely to do something than say something.

Encouragement, however, needs to be spoken. This may explain in part the results of a study done on doctors who are frequently sued for malpractice. Researchers at Vanderbilt University say, "The main difference between doctors who get sued a lot and those who don't isn't the quality of their medicine." Of 898 women who filed malpractice suits, one-third complained that their physicians "spent less than ten minutes on average during a visit."[3] In their high-pressured lives, many doctors often don't take time to affirm verbally what is important to their patients.

Like it or not, men are much the same way around the house. We frequently fail to communicate with our wives and our children. We are not talkers, and our families wonder why. They wonder if they do not please us. Even the family dog enjoys a word of affirmation occasionally. You can be the encourager in your home if you just do it, or in this case, just say it.

Undivided attention. Some days we need at least six pairs of hands. There just doesn't seem to be enough hours in the day to accomplish all the tasks people expect us to do. One of the ways men get more done is to do more than one thing at a time. I am as guilty of doing this as the next guy. While I have one project printing out on my computer, I am researching the next project and listening to the news at the same time. But this can be devastating to your role as encourager in the home.

A friend of mine thinks he's wasting time if he isn't doing at least two things at once. His wife, on the other hand, refuses to talk to him unless he gives her his total attention. That's understandable. When he splits his attention between her and something else, to her it implies she doesn't deserve his undivided attention. In a subtle way, it's an insult.

To be the encourager in your home requires setting aside other responsibilities and devoting yourself to the ministry of encouragement. Dad, those who are worthy of your encouragement are also worthy of your complete attention.

Eye contact. One of the first lessons students learn in their college speech or seminary preaching class is the importance of eye contact. As a preacher, I know the fastest way to lose an audience is not through an uninspiring sermon or faulty delivery but through limited eye contact.

Professors of homiletics have always urged their students to maintain good eye contact with their audience at any cost. "Eye contact between preacher and listener should be as intimate and continuous as possible," says one textbook.[4]

Maintaining eye contact with an audience is remarkably easy, however, compared with maintaining individual eye contact. Have you noticed how briefly we look into other people's eyes? The science of kinesics is the study of the relationship between nonlinguistic body motions, such as shrugs or eye movement, and communication. Scientists working in this field have learned that eye contact between two people in a normal conversation usually lasts only about a second before one or both look away.

Think of how furtively you look at strangers walking down the street. Your eye contact with them is only milliseconds. If you look into their eyes much more than that, they think you are staring at them.

And yet the eye has been called the window to our soul. Something special occurs when we give people eye contact. We show ourselves trustworthy. We open ourselves and show them our soul. We build a bridge of trust. They are more likely to believe we are being truthful with them as we seek to encourage them.

If you want to build a godly home, you need to look your family members in the eye while encouraging them. The eye communicates compassion, interest, concern, and a whole range of emotions. Your family needs to see your soul if they are to feel your heart. A world of encouragement can be communicated by the simple, sincere meeting of the eyes.

Loving touch. We Westerners are not touchy-feely people. We do not hold hands, give bear hugs, or embrace the way Europeans and others do. When was the last time you were greeted with a holy kiss?

Often I have walked down the streets of the Old City of Jerusalem and watched two Arab men holding hands as they walked ahead of me. Frequently they walk arm in arm. Every time I am in the Middle East, I am greeted by my friends with a hug and a light kiss on each cheek. When in Italy I am greeted with a hearty handshake and what I call a near-miss kiss; it comes close to being a kiss on each cheek, but it floats in the air instead.

These are cultural customs that many of us in the Western world are not comfortable with. Even in the United States our customs differ dramatically by region. Give someone a hug at church in the South and you are fellowshipping. Do that most places in the North and you get strange glances.

Touch has to be handled carefully in these days of sexual harassment and abuse. Dads especially need to be as wise as a serpent and as harmless as a dove. Touching a woman other than your wife or touching a child can raise questions about a man's fidelity or integrity. Nevertheless, if done appropriately, a loving touch to those in our family can be encouraging and healing.

When you are encouraging your son, putting your arm around his shoulder may mean more to him than you know. When you are encouraging your daughter, a gentle hug can affirm her value to you. When you are encouraging your wife, the loving touch of holding her hand or a tender kiss can communicate more encouragement than all the words you can think of.

Be careful and comfortable with what you do, but don't let the world rob your family of the loving touch they need and desire from you. After all, real men should be able to show their feelings too. You can be the man of the house without being cold and distant.

Judicious confrontation. Earlier I said that people in the throes of discouragement need friends, not critics. That's true. But sometimes the most loving thing you can do for a family member is gently, lovingly confront him about his faults.

The Bible is filled with advice about exhorting those who step out of line. Paul counseled the Thessalonian elders: "Now we exhort you, brethren, warn those who are unruly, comfort the fainthearted, uphold the weak, be patient with all" (1 Thessalonians 5:14). The unruly are those who have become disorderly or who have stepped out of line. The Romans used this Greek word (*ataktos*) of soldiers who broke rank. The word also was used of those who did not show up for work.

We've all had family members who could be described as unruly. Our son stepped out of line; our daughter stayed out too late; someone didn't show up for dinner on time. These are common, everyday occurrences. But they provide the man of the house with an opportunity to be an encourager rather than a critic.

Are you an encourager or a critic to your family? Do you admonish them when they break the rules, or do you annihilate them? In a world where families are so fragile, we need more encouragers.

WHO NEEDS IT?

Who needs encouragement? We all do. Perhaps the only exceptions are the Vulcan Commander Spock and the android Mr. Data. The rest of us have feelings and therefore need encouragement.

No man in Scripture provides a better example of an encourager than Jose (or Joseph). This man was so gifted at encouraging his friends and family that most people know him only by the nickname the apostles gave him—Barnabas (Acts 4:36).

Nicknames usually reflect more about us than our given names do. For example, you don't normally find someone six foot, six inches tall called "Shorty." Nor do you find someone five foot, two inches, weighing two hundred pounds nicknamed "Slim." Nicknames accurately reflect the way other people view us. "Red," "Stretch," "Junior," "Sweetheart"—all these reveal the perceptions others have about us.

The nickname Barnabas means "Son of Encouragement." Obviously, this man of the house had learned how to be a world-class encourager. His life teaches us about the people who need our encouragement.

Barnabas knew how to encourage his fellow Christians. In Acts 11, the message of salvation through Jesus Christ reached the non-Jewish population of Antioch. God's Spirit opened their hearts and a great number believed. When the Christian leaders in Jerusalem heard this, they sent Barnabas to see what was happening. Verse 23 says, "When he came and had seen the grace of God, he was glad, and *encouraged* them all that with purpose of heart they should continue with the Lord." Barnabas knew that Christians need encouragement as much as anyone else.

Dad, if you are the head of a Christian family, consider yourself fortunate. You occupy a position of great privilege and responsibility. Yet don't think your challenges are any less. Your family needs megabytes of encouragement just like other families do, and they are looking to you to provide it.

Urge your family to discover and use their spiritual gifts. You are in a prime position—in daily contact with your wife and children—to discern how they may be gifted. Read through passages such as Romans 12:6–8 and 1 Corinthians 12:7–10 to familiarize yourself with the spiritual gifts. Watch for these gifts to appear in your family. Then spend the time necessary to encourage your loved ones to use them.

Be an encourager to your wife in her spiritual walk. If your family includes small children, she will need your concerned help to find a time for daily meeting with her Lord. Provide her with opportunities for spiritual refreshment both in the home and outside. This may entail baby-sitting or hiring a baby-sitter while she attends church functions. It also means keeping in touch with where she is spiritually and what she might need to grow in her relationship with Christ. Encourage her to be the woman God created her to be, to pursue interests He has placed within her, and then support her.

The Lincoln Journal Star featured an article about a Grand Island, Nebraska, woman named Judy O'Sullivan. At the gentle urging of her husband, Judy agreed to take a college course. Seven years, two children, and countless late nights later, Judy graduated *summa cum laude* with a business degree from the University of Nebraska.

When asked what role her husband played in her success, Mrs. O'Sullivan said that she got a lot of help from her husband, Rod. He cooked the meals and took care of the kids so she could concentrate on her school work. He also provided "unspoken words of encouragement," she said. Whenever she had hours of homework left to do at bedtime, Rod would come down into the basement with a cup of coffee or a plate of cheese and crackers. That's being the encourager in the home.

TAKE A CHANCE

There is risk involved in encouragement. People sometimes disappoint us after we have spent a lot of time and effort to encourage them, which makes us occasionally wonder if giving encouragement is worth it. The way Barnabas encouraged others, however, helps us understand the value of that risk.

In Acts 9, the rabbi Saul (who later became the apostle Paul) encountered a bright light on the road to Damascus. Out of that light, Jesus spoke and Saul became a new man. After a time, Saul returned to Jerusalem, where people knew him only as the persecutor of the church. Even the disciples found it difficult to believe that Saul had become a new creature in Christ. It was too big of a change to readily accept.

Barnabas, however, was willing to take a chance. Scripture records, "But Barnabas took him and brought him to the apostles. And he declared to them how he had seen the Lord on the road, and that He had spoken to him, and how he had preached boldly at Damascus in the name of Jesus" (Acts 9:27). Paul's conversion was legitimate, but only Barnabas was willing to take the risk of finding out. Everyone else waited for Paul to prove himself.

I recently read that 95 percent of prospective jurors in a famous murder case indicated they disagreed with one of the main tenets of American jurisprudence—innocent until proven guilty. Unfortunately, that happens in our homes too. Too often we assume guilt rather than innocence. How encouraging it is to find that home is a place of refuge, a place where people think the best of us, like Barnabas thought of Saul. How refreshing it is to find families where the focus is on what people are doing right.

A "Dennis the Menace" cartoon shows Dennis in his mother's embrace. The caption has Dennis saying, "I had to come home. I needed someone on my side." That's the way God wants our homes to be.

This doesn't mean we condone sin. It means we assume our loved ones are innocent until proven guilty. We take a chance on them. We stick with them through thick and thin. If they are proven guilty, we still stick with them and encourage them to change and do what's right.

We all need someone on our side. That's why we need dads who are encouragers in their homes.

ENCOURAGE THE DEFEATED

One of the most memorable television commercials I ever saw depicted a teenage boy who had just lost a big game. His father came alongside, walked with him in silence for a few minutes, and then said, "Want a Life Saver, son?" This commercial is memorable because it portrays one of those life moments when we need an encourager.

Barnabas also knew how to encourage those who were failures. Acts 13 records Paul's first missionary journey. Among those who accompanied him were Barnabas and a young man named John Mark (Acts 13:5), a relative of Barnabas. Later John Mark left the group halfway through their journey (v. 13). He is the first recorded missionary failure. But that didn't deter Barnabas. When Paul decided to return to the churches they had visited earlier (Acts 15:36), Barnabas wanted to take John Mark with them again. Paul refused. The resulting disagreement caused these two friends and fellow workers to go their separate ways.

Barnabas felt so strongly about encouraging failures that he was willing to split with a dear friend and colleague to do so. Encouragement was such a part of his nature that he wouldn't quit even when faced with a deserter like John Mark. But with time things change, and so did John Mark. This young failure, having been encouraged by Barnabas, went on to walk with the Lord and write the Gospel of Mark. Even Paul changed his opinion of the young man (2 Timothy 4:11). This all happened because someone chose to encourage instead of condemn.

There are times when people fail you. Even your own family will disappoint you sometimes. We must resist the urge to "write them off." God wants to use them in your life to build perseverance and patience. He wants to use you in their life to change, challenge, and strengthen them.

WHAT IT TAKES

To encourage others you must begin by honestly looking at yourself. What kind of a person are you? A critical person has an uncanny ability to see everybody's faults but his. An encourager is aware of people's faults but has an equally uncanny ability to choose not to dwell on them.

When anyone would approach D. L. Moody with a word of criticism about another person, he would reply, "Right now I'm having so much trouble with D. L. Moody that I don't have time to find fault with the other fellow."

An encourager chooses to see the positives in his family. Dads who are encouragers do not have perfect families, but those families do have positive dads. The choice is yours, Dad. You can uplift a discouraged son or deepen his discouragement. You can encourage your wife or put her down. You can be a world-class encourager to your family, or you can cover their hopes and dreams like a wet blanket.

An encourager is not the same as a Pollyanna. This expression comes from a book written by Eleanor Porter. The heroine, a young girl named Pollyanna, always played the "glad game." She refused to see the negative in anything but always focused on the positive. But this denies reality. A better approach is to be aware of the problems but focus on the solutions. Recognize the difficulties but plan to overcome them. Acknowledge the negatives but emphasize the positives.

Two boys were overheard on the playground discussing a classmate. One said, "He's no good at sports."

The other replied, "Yes, but he never cheats when he plays."

The critical one retorted, "He isn't a very good student either."

"True, but he tries hard."

"Well," said the boy with the sharp tongue, "have you noticed how worn-out his clothes are?"

"I have, but I've also noticed how clean they are."

Which one was the encourager? Which one is most like you?

THE CONSEQUENCES OF BEING AN ENCOURAGER

There are surprising consequences to living life as an encourager. The most apparent benefits arise from within ourselves.

The Book of Proverbs says, "A merry heart makes a cheerful countenance, but by sorrow of the heart the spirit is broken" (15:13). "All the days of the afflicted are evil, but he who is of a merry heart has a continual feast" (v. 15). "A merry heart does good, like medicine, but a broken spirit dries the bones" (17:22).

The benefits of an encouraging outlook on life are corroborated by science. A group of psychologists from Bonn, Germany, discovered that men who kiss their wives every morning have fewer automobile accidents, miss less work because of sickness, and tend to live longer. All this from a kiss. What's the connection? The man who kisses his wife every morning is most likely to start the day with a positive attitude. (Perhaps a good-bye kiss in the morning is a way to encourage the encourager in the home.)

The encourager not only lives longer, but he also lives more prosperously. One study found that men who view life positively earn 20 to 30 percent more each year than men with a negative attitude. Charles Schwab exemplified this attitude. He was one of the first men to earn a million dollars a year, and he also was an encourager. Schwab claimed his success had nothing to do with a knowledge of his field. In fact, he freely admitted he had people working for him who knew more than he did. He earned what he did primarily because of his ability to deal with people.

Schwab said, "I consider my ability to arouse enthusiasm among other people the greatest asset I possess, and the way to develop the best that is in a man is by appreciation. There is nothing else that so kills the ambitions of man as criticisms from his superiors. I never criticize anyone. I believe in giving a man incentive to work. So I am anxious to praise but loath to find fault. If I like anything, I am hearty in my approbation and lavish in my praise." That's having the attitude of encouragement!

Most important of all, encouragement changes the lives of others. Being an encourager can cause you to be the most significant change agent your family has seen.

In the children's story *Little Lord Fauntleroy*, a young boy of about seven goes to live with his crotchety, old grandfather. The elderly man is known in the community for being mean and selfish. But the boy appears oblivious to that. Over and over again he tells his grandfather, "Oh, Grandpa, how people must love you! You're so good and kind in all you do." Even when the grandfather was disagreeable, his grandson saw the best in everything he did. Finally, the man no longer could resist the boy's influence and in time became the unselfish and kind person his grandson thought him to be.

Our family members have a will of their own. We cannot guarantee a change in their lives such as the grandfather experienced. Still, it is more likely to occur in the context of positive encouragement than in negative criticism. Your family gets ground into the dirt sufficiently by the world; make home a place where they can be lifted up, brushed off, and encouraged.

William Barclay wrote, "One of the highest of human duties is the duty of encouragement. It is easy to pour cold water on their enthusiasm; it is easy to discourage others. The world is full of discouragers. We have a Christian duty to encourage one another. Many a time a word of praise or thanks or appreciation or cheer has kept a man on his feet."[5] I might add, what's true for a man is true for a wife and a teenager and a child.

Dad, when your children grow up, what will they remember about you? Will it be that you never had a good word for them? Will it be that you were so intent on perfection that you never encouraged them right where they were? Perhaps we all need to take a phrase from the Kansas state song, "O give me a home . . . where never is heard a discouraging word."

Let's determine to be a Barnabas. As the man of the house, be a lightning rod of encouragement. Draw your family to yourself and send them away charged with courage.

[1] Zig Ziglar, "See You at the Top" (tape), Fullerton, Calif., 1985.

[2] Lawrence J. Crabb Jr. and Dan B. Allender, *Encouragement: The Key to Caring* (Grand Rapids, Mich.: Zondervan, 1984), p. 15.

[3] Jerry E. Bishop, "Studies Conclude Doctors' Manner, Not Ability, Results in More Lawsuits," *The Wall Street Journal*, November 23, 1994.

[4] Webb B. Garrison, *The Preacher and His Audience* (Eastwood, N.J.: Fleming H. Revell Co., 1954), p. 236.

[5] William Barclay, *Letter to the Hebrews* (Philadelphia: The Westminster Press, 1976), pp. 122–123.

Conclusion

ARE YOU MAN ENOUGH?

A fourth grade Sunday school teacher wanted to see how much his pupils knew. He asked, "What did God have to say about marriage?" A little boy in the back row piped up, "Father, forgive them for they know not what they do."

I know that was true of me when I was first married. I had no idea what all was involved in being the head of the home. Perhaps you were the same.

A young man went to the pastor of a large church for advice about a marriage proposal he was going to offer that evening to his girlfriend. Unknown to him, the pastor had just placed an ad for a nanny to help his wife take care of the kids. When the young man rang the doorbell, the minister answered. Before the boy could get beyond, "Reverend, I came to see you about . . . ," the pastor began to drill him.

"Can you cook, change diapers, clean house, shovel walks, take care of the finances, and entertain children?"

"Wait a minute," the young man gasped. "I just came by to find out if I should propose tonight. But if it's that much work, I'm not interested!"

Building a godly home is a lot of hard work. It might be true, as some believe, that marriages are made in heaven, but all the kinks have to be worked out here on earth. Then in a matter of a few years, most marriages have further "complications"—they're called children. Suddenly, the man of the house is no longer just a husband; he is also a father.

A friend gave me a drawing depicting the ultimate father. He wears a hard hat because he goes to the school of hard knocks. One ear has a plug that screens out loud music, while the other is attached to a phone so that he is always in touch with what's happening. His nose is large so he can sniff out personal needs, and his eyes bulge so he can see all that goes on. His shoulders are padded and always available to lean on, while his knees are protected so he can spend lots of time in prayer. His feet are shod in tennis shoes so he can excel in all sports, and his watch indicates he has time for everybody.

Fortunately, God doesn't want the husband/father to be Superman; He just wants him to be a godly man. This brings us back to where we started: obedience.

During the Christmas season, a burglar in Grand Junction, Colorado, got stuck twenty feet down inside the chimney of a pawn shop. During the two days he spent waiting for someone to rescue him, he had plenty of time to think about how uncompromising chimneys can be. A thirty-inch flue just won't accept a forty-inch waist.

We need to have that same uncompromising attitude. When faced with the overwhelming task of being the kind of man God calls you to be, you may be tempted to cut some corners. But you can't do that and still be a real man. Resist the temptation!

Do you want to build a godly home? Then you need to be a man of God. Such a man does not attempt to alter God's blueprint for manhood; he seeks to follow it. It's not that God is hard or a cruel taskmaster; He simply knows what it takes to be a real man. It is a challenge for us to fulfill that role, but our Heavenly Father offers help.

Most basic, He offers salvation through His Son, Jesus Christ. Salvation is not concerned with rituals; it's a matter of relationships. Sin breaks our relationship with God. We cannot have fellowship with Him until our debt for sin is paid. When we surrender our lives to Christ, the merits of His death upon the cross are applied to our lives and our sin debt is erased. We are reunited with God the Father and are able to enjoy all the blessings that flow from such a relationship.

Furthermore, as one who has experienced a spiritual new birth, you can draw supernatural strength and wisdom from God's Holy Spirit. When the disciples were preparing to fan the Gospel flame throughout a world darkened by sin, Jesus "commanded them not to depart from Jerusalem, but to wait for the Promise of the Father . . . [for] you shall receive power when the Holy Spirit has come upon you; and you shall be witnesses to Me in Jerusalem, and in all Judea and Samaria, and to the end of the earth" (Acts 1:4, 8).

Men who want to fulfill God's calling to be "real men" need to walk in the power of His Spirit. God has called you to a position that you cannot live up to on your own. Either you daily seek the power that comes through the Holy Spirit, or you fail.

This means keeping short accounts with God. When you displease Him, you must go before His throne of mercy and confess your sins.

Unconfessed sin clogs up the channel between God's Spirit and you. Confession means agreeing with God that what you are doing is wrong. The apostle John wrote, "If we confess our sins, He is faithful and just to forgive us our sins and to cleanse us from all unrighteousness" (1 John 1:9).

The satisfaction of being a real man can be discovered nowhere else but in God our Maker. Fulfillment can be found in no other source. Our confidence is in God's faithfulness. Numbers 23:19 says, "God is not a man, that He should lie, nor a son of man, that He should repent. Has He said, and will He not do? Or has He spoken, and will He not make it good?"

Wealth does not satisfy. Many men have tried that route and all have failed. William Borden was the heir to the multimillion-dollar Borden estate. But all the money that could have been his didn't deaden the pain he felt when he thought of the spiritual needs of those in faraway places. He gave himself wholly to serve the Lord as a missionary. He wrote in his journal:

> Say "no" to self, "yes" to Jesus every time . . . In every man's heart there is a throne and a cross. If Christ is on the throne, self is on the cross; and if self, even a little bit, is on the throne, Jesus is on the cross in that man's heart . . . Lord, I take my hands off, as far as my life is concerned. I put Thee on the throne of my life. Change, cleanse, use me as Thou shalt choose.

Borden set out for China to preach the Gospel but never made it. On a stopover in Egypt he contracted spinal meningitis and died less than a month later. On a note found by his bedside were scrawled these words: "No reserves, no retreat and no regrets."[1]

He sounds like a real man to me!

Dave Dravecky was an all-star pitcher for the San Francisco Giants. Dravecky loved baseball. As he said, "There on the mound, throwing my pitches, I was able to completely control the mood and the tempo of the game. It was an incredible feeling of power."[2]

But just before the playoffs in the fall of 1987, Dravecky found a small lump on his left arm. Almost a year later it was diagnosed as a low-grade malignancy. On October 7, 1988, half of his deltoid muscle was removed to prevent the cancer from spreading. Despite the best efforts of his doctors, the cancer returned, and in November 1989

Dravecky was forced to retire from baseball. On June 18, 1990, his arm and part of his shoulder were amputated. His response? "Perhaps most of all, I've learned to put my life in God's hands."[3]

He sounds like a real man to me!

"Tough, wily, nasty and tenaciously loyal to Richard Nixon" was *TIME* magazine's description of Chuck Colson. Friends and foes alike called him the "Hatchet Man." President Nixon knew that if he needed a job done, he could count on Colson to do it. He was one of the president's closest confidants and wielded more power than any of the other presidential advisors.

But his power didn't satisfy. Now, years after the Watergate scandal, Colson comments, "I remembered how I had once been caught up in the power games of the White House. I thought that domination on the political scene, money and prestige would provide life's fulfillment. But the quest for power is like the dryness of a man drinking salt water. The more he drinks, the more he demands. His thirst is never quenched."[4]

Imprisoned for his part in the Watergate break-in and cover-up, Colson found the real way to satisfy his thirst. He found Jesus Christ. From his prison experience and his new-found faith in Christ was born Prison Fellowship, dedicated to ministering to men and women in prison all over the world.

He sounds like a real man to me!

Money doesn't satisfy; fame doesn't satisfy; power doesn't satisfy. It takes much more than that. It takes God.

Real men are not the macho stereotypes we see on television. Real men are not motivated by greed, power, or any other vice. Real men, men of God, go forward with a new birth (born from above), a new spirit (the Holy Spirit), and a new confidence (the faithfulness of God). They know what God looks for in a man, and they want to be that man.

Do you want to build a godly home? Then you need to be a God-ignited, God-enthused man. A man who is willing to follow God's blueprint for manhood. Will you be that man? Don't build just any home; build a godly home.

---

[1] Del Fehsenfeld Jr., "From the Director," *Spirit of Revival*, April 1986, p. 1.

[2] Dave Dravecky, *Comeback* (Grand Rapids, Mich.: Zondervan, 1990), p. 26.

[3] Ibid., p. 248.

CONCLUSION

[4] Charles Colson, "My Journey from Watergate," *Christianity Today*, September 13, 1993, p. 96.